CHUCK GARRISON'S MODERN WESTERN

BASS

FISHING

CHUCK GARRISON'S MODERN WESTERN BASS FISHING

Photographs by the Author

CHRONICLE BOOKS
SAN FRANCISCO

DEDICATION

To Mom and Dad, who somehow managed
to keep me out of trouble as a youngster
by placing a fishing rod in my hand.

Cover photograph by Dave Lite.

Library of Congress Cataloging in Publication Data

Garrison, Chuck.
Modern Western bass fishing.

1. Black bass fishing. 2. Fishing—The West.
I. Title.
SH681.G35   799.1'58   78-1613
ISBN 0-87701-110-9

Chronicle Books
870 Market Street
San Francisco, CA 94102

Contents

Foreword   7

Introduction   11

About This Book   17

Chapter 1:   Tackle for Western Bass   19

Chapter 2:   The Bass Fishing Machine   36

Chapter 3:   The Art of Artificials   42

Chapter 4:   Fishing With Wigglies   65

Chapter 5:   Western Bass Structures   73

Chapter 6:   Tips for Taking Western Bass   79

Chapter 7:   Bass Waters of the West   85

Chapter 8:   In Search of the Superbass   95

Chapter 9:   A Western Pro Talks Bass   101

Chapter 10:   For Better Bass Photos   109

A Final Thought   116

Acknowledgements   117

Foreword

Over the past decade, the most significant change in United States · sportfishing has been the increase in popularity of the freshwater bass.

The initial upsurge in angler enthusiasm for the noble *Micropterus* began in the late 1960s in the Deep South, given impetus, no doubt, by the national Bass Anglers Sportsman Society (BASS), since there the native largemouth bass has always ranked as the number-one game fish. That enthusiasm, however, was not confined below the Mason-Dixon line for long—interest in black bass fishing soon spread like prairie fire to all corners of the nation, including our own Western states.

The increased popularity of bass angling in the West is exemplified in California, where the annual catch rate in the 1970s has been more than *double* what it was in the 1950s. In addition, upwards of 20,000 avid, Golden State anglers now belong to organizations which deal *exclusively* with black bass fishing. Despite the fact that California and the West generally are—and always will be—known as good trout country, the organized bass fishermen far outnumber their trout fishing counterparts. Why? I suspect that many bass fishermen are a different breed, preferring club meetings, tournament fishing, seminars, and the other activities which make up the organized club scene, in contrast to the seclusion sought by many trout enthusiasts.

Black bass have been introduced into a variety of habitats in the West: the warmer lowland streams and irrigation canals, farm ponds, natural lakes, and even the upstream reaches of estuaries such as the extensive Sacramento-San Joaquin Delta. But it is in the large, manmade warmwater reservoirs that *Micropterus* has really flourished. Without these large reservoirs, black bass fishing could not have become a significant attraction in the West. (For the record, I should point out that the creation of some good bass reservoirs has had serious impact on anadromous salmon and steelhead fisheries and also on critical wildlife habitat, by changing bodies of water from rivers into lakes and flooding adjacent land. In the future, water development projects should be planned to avoid the loss of valuable fish and wildlife resources.)

In California and, I suspect, in other Western states as well, the nearly explosive increase in fishing pressure and its possible effects on bass populations initially worried the Department of Fish and Game. Annual harvests in the more popular lakes spurted to surprisingly high rates. Then evidence of a declining catch surfaced, and in some lakes an alarming increase in the harvest of bass under 12 inches in length was noted. State biologists began to discuss the possibility that the bass resource might be in trouble.

Normally, when a fish and wildlife problem arises, a new study must be designed and funded to solve the problem. Fortunately, in California, reservoirs had been under investigation for several years, because fishery managers had long recognized that these waters offered the most promise for meeting future angling demands.

Consequently, when concern over some bass populations rose, an impressive amount of information was already available regarding reservoir fisheries in general and the black bass fisheries in particular. The major problems for black bass and potential solutions to them were promptly identified.

The major problems for black bass in California reservoirs, and in many instances in other Western states, are the following: (1) overharvest; (2) shoreline habitat loss; (3) water level fluctuations; and (4) competition between threadfin shad, an important forage fish, and young-of-the-year bass.

Research has shown that overharvest can be effectively controlled by imposing a minimum size limit. In California, 12-inch size limits are being applied selectively to waters where the take of small bass has been excessive. And while our experiments in Southern California with Florida-strain largemouths have shown this type of bass to be definitely resistant to overharvest, widespread transplants of Floridas to Northern California have been deemed inadvisable since the winter mortality of this subtropical race of bass seems to be greater than that of the more widespread "northern" bass.

As for shoreline vegetation, *new* reservoirs typically have ample vegetation to produce favorable spawning habitat for bass and insure a good survival rate for young fish. As reservoirs age, however, most of this shelter washes out and, as a result, bass reproduction declines.

Still, there is much hope. For example, experimental work has shown that the planting of certain willow species in the water-level fluctuation zone of reservoirs greatly improves bass spawning and survival. This is probably the most significant recent finding in bass research in the West. We now have a means of management that really works and have begun planning a program to develop shoreline habitat in older lakes.

Size limits and shoreline habitat development are only two examples of measures which can enhance bass populations. Other promising measures are being evaluated, and those of us who are responsible for the management of the public's black bass resources are confident that the future of Western bass angling is bright indeed.

G. W. (George) McCammon
Chief, Inland Fisheries Branch
California Department of Fish and Game

*This angler releases a small bass so
that it can grow and provide another thrill
for someone else in the future.*

*Professional tournament bass fishing in the 1960s
provided much recognition to the sport and brought
many changes in tackle and fishing techniques.*

Introduction

"The Black Bass is eminently an American fish, and has been said to be representative in his characteristics. He has the faculty of asserting himself and making himself completely at home wherever placed. He is plucky, game, brave and unyielding to the last when hooked. He has the arrowy rush and vigor of the Trout, the untiring strength and bold leap of the Salmon, while he has a system of fighting tactics peculiarly his own."

—James A. Henshall
Book of the Black Bass, 1881

It would be an understatement to say that the sport of bass fishing has changed drastically in the last decade.

It wasn't too long ago—in the early 1960s—that many anglers were still "traditional" bass fishermen. They used many techniques and much tackle which, except for occasional improvements such as fiberglass rods and monofilament lines, had seen little basic modification since the turn of the century. Topwater lures, for example, were still very popular scarcely 10 years ago; fishermen concentrated their fishing in water less than 20 feet deep, seldom venturing very far from shore; and mostly plug-type lures lined the trays of many tackle boxes.

Until recently, few fishermen really understood much about the behavior of bass or the factors affecting bass habitat. Except being more vulnerable in the spring spawning season, bass were thought to be difficult to catch consistently; they were "too smart" to catch the rest of the year, according to many fishermen. That minority of hardcore bass fanciers who did somehow manage year-around to take impressive stringers of fish were thought to possess a "secret" spot, a "mysterious" method, or a "hot" lure which they wouldn't divulge.

Until the Age of Enlightened Bass Tactics, persistence alone was frequently the backbone of the average bass angler's success. A typical bass angling day of the early '60s involved simple strategy: Concentrate on the early morning and late afternoon periods, fish the shoreline, cast to visible bass cover, and crank a variety of plugs through the water so many times that sooner or later, often *later*, a bass would strike. If a guy took the limit, the fish were "hitting"; if he took a few, fishing was "slow." He seldom considered other techniques, types of lures, and bass habitat.

Then something happened.

In the mid-1960s a revolution began. Bass fishing was transformed nationwide, principally due to: (1) the formation of the Bass Anglers Sportsman Society; (2) the increased popularity of and skill in using bottom-hugging lures like the plastic worm and the leadhead jig; (3) the introduction of sophisticated electronic fishing aids; (4) the design and manufacture of sleek, high-powered, highly functional "bass boats"; and (5) the rapid growth of both local and regional bass fishing clubs. Beginning in the Deep South, these changes also affected the Western bass fisherman.

This transformation began in 1968 when Ray Scott of Montgomery, Alabama, came up with an idea to unite bass fishermen nationwide, something never attempted. Scott's idea was to offer anglers membership in the Bass Anglers Sportsman Society (which, not surprisingly, has the acronym BASS), an organization which holds major, cash-payoff fishing tournaments. In addition, BASS also publishes the first major magazine devoted exclusively to freshwater bass angling; promotes the formation and affiliation (to BASS) of local bass clubs; plays an active role in bass conservation and management programs; and creates "superstars" of bass fishing, via the national BASS "Tournament Trail," similar to the superstars of baseball, basketball or football.

Scott is generally credited with sponsoring the first big-money bass fishing tourney in the United States—the 1967 All-American Invitational Bass Tournament at Beaver Lake, Arkansas. Although he reportedly *lost* $600 as the promoter of the event, the enthusiastic response to this $5000-purse contest helped convince Scott to form the Bass Anglers Sportsman Society.

Scott was overwhelmed by support from the bass fishing public. People from all over the country joined BASS, read Scott's *Bassmaster* magazine, outfitted themselves with the latest gear, exchanged fishing information, interested others in joining BASS, and formed local bass clubs of their own. (Information regarding membership in BASS may be obtained by writing: Post Office Box 3044, Montgomery, Alabama 36109.)

Today the success of BASS is obvious: it boasts over 270,000 members; 1,962 BASS-affiliated clubs exist at this writing; its professional tournament circuit offers $500,000 in cash prizes; and its annual tournament trail ends in a "world series"-type competition—the annual BASS Masters Classic—which alone offers $50,000 in awards.

But organized, competitive bass fishing isn't for everyone. Cast-for-cash tournaments have come in for their share of criticism, mostly from people who believe that fishing should be a slower-paced and less competitive sport, one not influenced by big-money payoffs. And that's fine. Fishing is, after all, different things to different people. Personally, I find fishing to be good therapy since it offers me a chance to relax, to contemplate, and to generally enjoy the out-of-doors. For myself, I don't care for tournament competition. I would, however, be one of the first to point out that organized, tournament-style bass fishing has long supported the conservation of our largemouth bass resource. Scott's group, for example, has been the long-time sponsor of a "Don't Kill Your Catch" program which encourages the catching and releasing of bass. The BASS ethic is also apparent in the point system of their tournaments which award bonus points for fish weighed alive (then released back into the tournament lake) and their requirement that all tourney boats have aerated livewells to hold fish.

The success of Scott's catch-and-release philosophy has been exceptional. Today, after nearly 50 national BASS events, more than 80 percent of the total catch has been returned alive to the water. According to BASS officials, 8,005 fishermen accounted for 51,736 released bass in 47 tournaments, with a loss of only 12,293 fish, many of which succumbed while more effective catch-and-release techniques were still being refined.

As for the charge that tournament fishing places undue pressure on a bass lake, scientific studies so far cannot substantiate such claims. In fact, so-called pro bass fishermen often fare no better than the average guy in catching bass: The average catch for BASS tournament contestants to date has been *only 2.6 bass per day*.

Even Ray Scott, however, had little vision of what the formation of BASS would do to Bassdom, USA. The founding of his group met with such success that BASS received much exposure to the general fishing public through several national and regional outdoor publications. Suddenly *Micropterus salmoides* became the "in" fish of the times, and a jacket bearing bass fishing tackle patches became a status symbol to its owner. As a result of the interest generated by BASS and the media, fishing tackle manufacturers soon began realizing that they had a tremendous potential market, and a multitude of tackle developments emerged.

One of these was the fraudulent nightcrawler.

Fake nightcrawlers (first made of rubber and later molded of plastic) had actually already been in use for several years, since Nick Creme of the Creme Lure Company developed his original "rubber worms." But "the worm," as some anglers call it, had remained a relatively well-kept secret of an inner circle of bass experts; the lure requires a certain finesse to master its retrieve, and many fishermen tried plastic worms and gave up too quickly. The artificial 'crawlers thus remained a greatly underutilized bass catching device, and this, no doubt, extended the lives of a lot of bass.

Then, the Bass Anglers Sportsman Society began to publicize the effectiveness of this lure and the methods of fishing it correctly. More anglers learned to use plastic worms, lure production increased and, today, the manufacture of the wiggly, molded creature is a multimillion dollar business. Not only are plastic worms now offered in a variety of lengths, patterns, and colors; they also come in such fashions as curly tails, twister tails, straight tails, twin tails, floaters, sinkers, ringed worms, bubble worms, and many soft-lure offshoots resembling lizards, waterdogs, water snakes, grubs, and salamanders. And bass love them all.

About the time that BASS was growing and plastic-worm fishing was increasing, another event greatly changed traditional bass fishing.

Carl Lowrance introduced his "little green box" to the fishing fraternity.

Inside the metal box was a piece of electronic wizardry manufactured by Lowrance Electronics of Tulsa, Oklahoma, and marketed under the catchy name of "Fish Lo-K-Tor."

This device was an electronic depthfinder, a unit which operated on the principle of sonar. It sent out soundwaves which bounced back from lake-bottom structures and were picked up on a transducer which changed the soundwave impulses into light signals on a depth-graduated dial. Thus, an angler switched on his Fish Lo-K-Tor, watched the depth-marked facedial on his little green box, and received information about the terrain of the area below him. (The first units introduced by Lowrance were portable, boxlike models in green, metal outer cases, hence the name.) The fisherman related this sonar information to what he knew about bass structure and preferred depths and, in many cases, found completely new fishing spots, skyrocketing his catches.

The single largest advantage of the Fish Lo-K-Tor and other depthfinders is the unit's ability to eliminate a lot of *unproductive* water from the bassman's search. By means of the pattern of light, bright blips on its facedial, the Lo-K-Tor, for instance, indicates which areas are too deep and lacking in oxygen or too muddy or too flat to fish. It reveals much understructure which could never be "charted" by human eyes. With the aid of electronics, the fisherman can find underwater islands, pinpoint ledges, and determine locations of old creek channels and long points running far out into a lake.

For a while, many of these structures proved to be "honey holes," the tournament fisherman's term for bonanza bass-fishing spots, until many more anglers outfitted themselves with depthfinders and found the same areas.

As a result of what electronic depthfinders revealed in the late 1960s about bass habitat, new theories of bass angling evolved—theories based on fishing deep-water structures—and, as a consequence, tackle manufacturers began to introduce specialized gear designed for this style of bassin'. Appearing in the angling arsenal were more refined bait-casting reels, many with improved casting capabilities; better drag mechanisms and faster gear ratios; special "worm" and "jig" rods adapted from the basic bait-casting design; plastic worm slip sinkers and specially shaped hooks; "rattle chambers" which, installed in plastic worms, created another dimension—noise—to attract the quarry; and a host of other innovations.

The popularity of depthfinders only served to *start* the sophisticated fishing-aids boom. Soon electronic water-temperature gauges and trolling motors found their way into an expanding marketplace, along with such elaborate devices as oxygen meters (which measure oxygen content in parts-per-million and relate PPM to bass oxygen requirements). Some observers were wondering if the modern day angler would soon be spending too much time adjusting dials, pressing buttons, and reading meters, leaving little time to enjoy fishing. Or if the rapid advances in electronic fishing would hurt the bass resource by making the fish too vulnerable to hook-and-line. Fortunately, neither has been the case so far.

The professional bass angler of the late 1960s was, himself, responsible for much change in fishing style. These first pros of the sport were not content to fish from old-style craft while competing in a big-money tournament which allowed only limited fishing time. After all, more *fishing* time and less *cruising* time meant better odds for finishing high in the point standings. So tourney competitors demanded faster boats; boats with lesser drafts to fish in shallow water; boats outfitted with elevated casting platforms and swivel seats, bow-mounted trolling motors and remote anchoring systems, ample tackle storage and livewells for the catch—all creating a more efficient fishing machine.

Based on designs resembling the old Southern "johnboat"—an open, low-gunwale, flat-bottomed craft—the first fiberglass "bass boats" began to emerge on the market. The Ranger boat, made by Forrest Woods of Flippin, Arkansas, was one of the first big-production bass boats and is still one of the finest and largest selling in the country. It is probable, of course, that the bass boat would have been introduced eventually, but the growth of BASS and tournament fishing, plus the tremendous exposure tourney fishing received in the large outdoor publications, definitely accelerated the development of the bass boat.

Once BASS was established and its ranks were swelling, other groups began to form similar organizations, each based on a series of tournaments. Project Sports, Inc., a Texas-based operation, was one of the early promoters, along with the Bass Casters Association, Ltd. (BCA) and the American Bass Fisherman (ABF). In 1972, Western fishermen who envisioned a regional group of their own formed the Western Bass Fishing Association.

"Western Bass," as it's commonly referred to by members, has as its goals the promotion of bass fishing *in the West*; the education of members in how to catch bass; and, through its various conservation programs, the preservation of good fishing in the future. Western Bass also sponsors a youth fishing program, holds various fishing seminars, and organizes a series of cash tournament events, as well as publishing both a quarterly magazine, *Western Bass Fishing*, and a monthly newsletter. (Information regarding membership in the Western Bass Fishing Association may be obtained by writing: Post Office Box 2027, Newport Beach, CA 92663.)

By 1977, in a region supposedly dominated by trout fishermen, Western Bass had attracted nearly 12,000 members. Smaller, affiliated groups were springing up in Western states, and California alone was home to over 200 individual bass clubs.

The Western boom had hit.

Tournaments ranging from small, intra-club affairs to a full-fledged extravaganza staged by Western Bass (the first annual Wahweap/Lake Powell Fall Classic, with a $50,000 full-slate purse) appeared with increasing frequency. Bass seminars and clinics, featuring big-name, pro bass anglers as guest speakers, became commonplace. Tackle dealers found the Western bass fisherman to be one of the most dedicated—and tackle-acquiring—individuals to possess a fishing license.

Today there is a real "bass belt" in the West, probably not as easily defined as that of the Deep South, but still a significant geographical area which has changed as a result of the bass boom. The bass fraternity now stretches along the coast from Washington and Oregon in the north and California in the south, and then east to Nevada, Arizona, New Mexico, and Utah. Bass fishing also is available in Montana, Colorado, Wyoming, and Idaho, but these four states offer mostly coldwater fisheries which place their angling emphasis on trout, salmon, and similar species.

To describe bass fishing in the West, the word *diverse* might well be used. Practically no other region sees such varied methods and topography. The Western bass angler chucks a chunk of pork rind alongside a lilypad bed in a Washington lake surrounded by timber; he drifts a live waterdog through the deep, crimson sandstone canyons of Lake Powell, formed by the sinuous Colorado River of the desert Southwest; he teases a plastic worm along the bed of a saucer-bottomed reservoir in Southern California, on the outskirts of the heavily populated city of San Diego, in the hope of catching a new world record. And his catch may range from a 5-pound "trophy" in Montana to a 15-pound "honorable-mention-only" in California's finest Florida-strain bass lakes.

As bass fishing has changed in the West, so have the bass. Today's breed of fish are believed by some biologists to be, if you will, more "educated" than those bass of a decade ago. Increased fishing pressure and better tackle have made the fish spookier, warier, and more difficult to catch. There are few undiscovered "hot spots" yet to be found, and the vast exchange of bass fishing knowledge through clubs and publications has upgraded the skill level of the serious bass fisherman.

"Now the dumbest bass in a school is the one who's only been hooked twice," said one of my close fishing friends. That pretty well sums up the competition.

Today's modern Western bass fisherman must have the proper fishing gear, must use the right techniques, and must own a tackle box full of *persistence* if he hopes to consistently catch bass.

That's what this book is all about.

About This Book

Since you are about to begin reading the first chapter of *Modern Western Bass Fishing*, I'd like to say a few things.

First, I am not an "expert" bass fisherman. To my way of thinking, *expert* is a term reserved for the most highly skilled technicians and, in many cases, is too loosely applied in the sport of fishing. Through no lack of desire, I still find myself contending with those fishing days which prove I don't know everything. Some days, in fact, I wonder if I know *anything*.

I fish in a boat, like you do; I tie on a hook, like you do; and I try to catch a fish, like you do. We may differ, however, in that I have the opportunity to fish *a lot*, because of my work, and I do seem to catch something over the "average" share of fish. Still, I've never yet met the pro who doesn't get blanked occasionally or outfished by a beginner.

One of the fascinating aspects of angling is that we don't know everything about the sport. I hope we never do. Consider what the state of the art would soon become if we *did* discover all the secrets of successful fishing —knowing precisely when and where to fish and what to tie on our lines —and if catching full, legal limits became a certainty every time. What challenge would be left? What would remain to be learned? I think man likes to fish for sport because sometimes he is right, and sometimes he is wrong, and when he is right it's fun. It is, as the saying goes, the *bad* days which make the good days *good*.

Second, while I'm not an expert, I have had considerable experience in the pursuit of largemouth bass. Because of my profession I've had opportunities to fish with some of the largest names in tournament bass fishing, both in the Bass Anglers Sportsman Society and the Western Bass Fishing Association, as well as several non-affiliated and highly skilled bassers.

The anglers I have known have varied from the ultralight-tackle specialist to the "grind 'em in" buff; from the live-bait fancier to the artificial-lure master; from the scientific analyzer to the common-sense practitioner. Most are highly successful with their own methods, and I've attempted to learn something from all of them, eventually incorporating that knowledge into my own bass fishing systems.

This brings up the question: which method and equipment are best for catching bass? The answer is *those which work best for you*. All of the many theories of bass fishing have some merit; what works consistently (plastic worm fishing, for example) for one angler may not work well for another who might be a live-bait specialist. Most of the difference, I feel, lies in the confidence a fisherman feels when he uses that type of gear which has become comfortable to him.

Third, in my value system, catching a bass on an artificial lure is more personally rewarding than catching a fish on live bait, *but* (I'd like to emphasize) using live bait is no disgrace. And I've taken my share of kidding for flinging live nightcrawlers, crawfish, or waterdogs. Some bass fishermen simply disdain the use of live wigglies, feeling that artificial lures are more challenging—sometimes so challenging, I feel, that you'd swear there wasn't a fish in the lake.

I feel it's important, on any given day, to give the fish what they *prefer*. If it happens to be a live bait, it matters little to me (I've seldom been ribbed while carrying a big stringer of bass past a near-fishless lure man). After all, the real fun starts *after* the rod bends; I would rather *catch* fish on live bait than cast all day using artificials without a strike. But you decide for yourself. You may prefer to limit your strategy to lures. Great. There is certainly room for both philosophies.

Fourth, the information in this book is a compilation of what I've managed to learn in 16 years as a regular fisherman and in the last 9 years, as an outdoor photojournalist who, as part of his work, has the immensely pleasurable assignment of fishing. No doubt there are many excellent techniques which I have not yet learned, and, too, you may disagree with some of the advice which is offered. Fishing is a sport filled with exceptions.

Finally, in my opinion, it's folly to attempt writing a book for the "expert" bass fisherman. The "expert" doesn't need a book or, at least, probably thinks he doesn't because he has already achieved proficiency. So this book is aimed at the other 90 percent of the fishing-license buyers.

If you consider yourself an average Western bass fisherman—one with some room for improvement—I think you'll find value in the following pages. There are no sure-fire methods or guaranteed gimmicks listed; at least I haven't found them yet. At best, proficient bass fishing is hard work.

On the other hand, if you'll make a sincere attempt to consider the tackle and techniques described here, you'll probably become a better angler.

Good Fishing,
Chuck Garrison

1

Tackle for Western Bass

If I were allowed only one word to describe proper bass fishing tackle, the type of tackle essential to *successful* angling, the answer would be simple: Q-u-a-l-i-t-y.

There is no substitute for quality.

Trying to become a good bass fisherman while using inferior tackle is about as effective as a skilled surgeon operating with a butter knife or a diamond cutter wielding a jackhammer. It just doesn't work. To limit yourself to less than quality tackle is to begin bass fishing at a distinct disadvantage.

It continually surprises me to see some anglers using gear that isn't even fit for teaching their youngsters how to fish.

I've seen enough inferior gear to know what unpleasant results it often produces: countless backlashes from reels which can't cast smoothly; broken lines from weak monofilament; unraveling rod windings, loose or broken guides, and "gutless" actions on poorly made rods; or hooks which pull out of inexpensively made (and priced) lures.

Like many others, I've learned the hard way—trying to cut corners. Several years ago, when I was first getting interested in bass fishing, I lost a fish I still haven't forgotten. Because of my "drugstore" rod and reel, I had very little control over the fish and, when it was finally right next to the boat, a sudden dash of the bass broke the "bargain" line. I had a good peek at that trophy before it escaped, however, and estimated its weight at over 10 pounds. When it broke the line, it practically broke my heart.

How much was that fish worth to me? Certainly much more than it would have cost me to buy dependable, high-grade line. But then, hindsight always has been more perceptive than foresight.

So, what is "quality" gear?

First, it's equipment which has proved itself over the years. Consider such major fishing tackle manufacturers as Fenwick, Garcia, Zebco, Shakespeare, Penn, Pflueger, Berkely, or Heddon. Each of these companies has been around for many years, perfecting its products and serving the needs of the fishing public. All are name-brand operations. And all of these manufacturers are striving for a share of the same buying public, so competition keeps their product standards high.

If you are in doubt about a certain tackle manufacturer, ask the advice of the most knowledgeable fisherman you know and benefit from his experience. Research your choices. In fact, ask *several* fishermen. Then compare their advice to the recommendations of *several* fishing tackle salespersons, not just one. When seeking store advice, you may find it helpful to consult those who work in *specialty shops*, stores which carry fishing tackle exclusively and are known to attract skilled anglers. Ask around a little and find out at which stores the good fishermen congregate.

Rule number one: Buy name-brand equipment. It will more than pay for itself through the years. You will have problems enough trying to catch bass, without using poor gear that further tips the odds in the fish's favor.

Many tackle manufacturers offer several lines or grades of equipment, much the same as General Motors offers automobiles ranging from Chevrolets to Cadillacs. In the American economic system you *do* get what you pay for. This applies whether you are buying a single lure for $2 or a new bass boat for $5,000.

When a company offers different grades of rods, reels, and lines, prices vary for a very good reason: the more expensive gear is made of higher quality components and may also cost more to manufacture, assemble, and quality-control the product.

Rule number two: Always buy the highest grade of quality you can afford, even if it means delaying purchases for a while until you can financially absorb the cost of better gear.

I would much rather own one or two excellent bass-fishing outfits than half a dozen cheap ones. The excellent ones will initially cost more on a per-unit basis, but will virtually last a lifetime. And they will be a pleasure to use. I have seen anglers lose all their composure when they lost a good fish, blaming their "bad luck" for the misfortune, when actually they should have blamed their tackle.

Is all this emphasis on quality really necessary? No, not at all if you're willing to put up with frustration while using the cheap stuff and willing to needlessly liberate a lot of fish. Including, of course, some truly handsome fish.

I think that answers the question.

Bait-Casting Gear

Look inside the West's·fleet of bass boats and you'll notice a preponderance of one certain type of fishing outfit—bait-casting rods and reels—and for very good reasons. Bait-casting outfits are versatile and rugged;

*Conventional bait-casting gear (above) and the
ultralight spinning outfit (below) are both important
in modern bass fishing.*

they cast well, handle a wide range of lines and lures, and offer unpar-
alleled control over a hooked fish.

It's true that a very few serious anglers use spin-casting rods and reels,
just as even fewer regularly use fly rods or ultralight spin rods, but it is the
bait-casting combo which has become the essential weapon in the skilled
bass angler's arsenal.

I've seen no statistics to verify this, but my observations in the field tell
me that the most popular equipment being used by *top notch* bass anglers
today is, in rank order: (1) bait-casting gear; (2) light- to medium-class,
open-face spinning gear; (3) ultralight-class, open-face spin tackle;
(4) spin-casting equipment; and (5) fly rod gear.

One reason bait-casting gear is so popular—and effective—is that the
bass is not an open-water fish. Bass are found around lake structures such
as rocks, brush, trees, and lily pads. This presents two problems to the
fisherman: (1) casting to areas where many line-fraying hazards are found
and (2) keeping a bass from reaching the safety of those hazards once it is
hooked.

Consider for a moment what would likely happen if the bass angler always used relatively light lines, say, 4- or 6-pound test. Working among brush, rocks, and other obstacles, he is going to miss his target occasionally and flip a certain number of lures into the snags. He is also going to lose a high percentage of those snagged lures because, more often than not, pulling on the light line will cause it to break before the lure comes free. (There are times when very light line may be an advantage in clear water, as we'll see later, but this isn't *usually* the case.)

In addition to losing a lot of lures on light line, he would also lose a lot of bass. Ol' *Micropterus* seems to instinctively know where the snags are located, and his unfailing logic tells him there's safety and escape in the snags. If there's a maze of tree limbs, rock outcroppings, water-lily beds, or old dock pilings nearby, he'll try to spurt into the middle of the mess.

To minimize the loss of lures and fish, lines testing from 12 to 17 pounds are usually used in bass fishing (again, there're exceptions we'll go into later), along with lures commonly ranging in weight from ⅜ to ¾ ounce. Bait-casting gear also handles these ranges of lines and lures most effectively. The bait-casting rod is stiff enough in action to cast the heavier lures and to turn a chugging bass which, by overpowering the lighter spinning gear, might otherwise reach safety.

Ask a professional, tournament bass angler why he prefers bait-casting equipment, and the answer you'll usually hear is "control."

First, control in casting is made easy because the bait-casting reel is a revolving spool-type reel, in contrast to the spinning reel which has a stationary spool. While the lure is sailing out toward the target, the experienced bait-caster can readily judge the lure's (or bait's) speed and trajectory, can instantly feed this information into his cerebral computer, and then, if necessary, can slow down the lure by lightly touching the revolving spool with the underside of his thumb, causing the lure to splash down on target. This "thumbing" or "feathering" of the line with the thumb is, I feel, the most accurate method of slowing down the lure after the cast is made by adjusting the cast in midair. This same type of effect can be achieved by using a finger to feather the line as it uncoils from a stationary, open-face reel spool, but not nearly so precisely as when using a bait-casting reel.

Unfortunately, no one has yet devised a trick to speed up a lure after an *under-powered* cast is made. It is better, obviously, to overcast than to undercast. Of course, it's best to learn to cast *precisely* on target, with no thumbing adjustment at all, and that comes with practice, practice, practice.

Bait-casting rods and reels also afford the angler another form of control—control of a hooked fish. Since bait-casting rods generally have stiffer actions (determined by the curve of the rod when strain is placed on the tip) and stouter tip sections than their spinning counterparts and since bait-casting equipment is ideal for up to 20-pound test lines, it's possible to apply more power against a fish when it is trying to head off in an opposite direction. Spinning gear, with its lighter lines and lighter rod actions, just isn't designed for this work.

Bait-casting gear looks heavier, feels heavier, and *is* heavier. To the novice, it could even appear unsporting. But considering the bass' knack for tangling or cutting lines in the brambles, the revolving-spool fraternity is only being realistic.

There is another advantage to bait-casting tackle. While fishing with plastic worms or leadhead jigs, the angler has a distinct advantage if he can "feel" a strike (often just the slightest twitch along the line) by "palming" the bait-casting reel in his left hand and holding the line between his left thumb and forefinger during the slow retrieve. As a result, a light tap-tap-tap, often characteristic of a shy biter, can be *felt* along the line. Since the bait-casting reel mounts *on top* of the reelseat, the palming and line-feeling can be accomplished easily by the same hand, something not possible with open-face spinning gear, which has the reel mounted *below* the rod, unless the angler also happens to be a contortionist.

Bait-casting gear is also rugged; it stands up well to the rigors of bass fishing. Being a rather loosely coordinated soul by nature, I've accidentally dropped or stepped on a bait-casting combo more than once, and usually it's come out none the worse. I can't say the same for spinning gear, which seems to have more breakable parts extending out from the reel, making them highly susceptible to mishap.

And now the hitch. After all, if bait-casting gear has such advantages for the bass chaser, why don't more *beginners* use this type of equipment?

Fear, frustration and patience are all part of the answer. Many beginners fear bait-casting tackle with good reason because they have visions of mounds of snarled line created by the nightmarish backlashes of a revolving spool. I know. I picked out my share of backlashes while I was learning. Until the mind, arm, wrist, and thumb develop a degree of interrelated finesse, backlashes will occur. Given a choice, most fishermen would rather fish than knit and beginners fear the thought of "knitting" out those snarls.

One way to overcome the frustration of the backlash is to start *slow*. Practice bait-casting with an experienced friend; have him show you the basic steps of casting. Forget about distance; that will come in time. Concentrate first on smoothness, on coordinating the proper back cast, the forward thrust, the release of the thumb on the spool, and then controlling the flight of the lure (and any possible override of the line) by lightly re-applying the thumb to the revolving spool. Smoothness is more important —far more important—than distance. Follow smoothness with accuracy.

Practice in your backyard. There are several targets you can use: a couple of old tires laid flat on the ground, a couple old hula-hoops, pieces of string curved to form circles on the grass, almost anything that presents a circular target into which the practice plug can fall.

*Bait-casting gear allows excellent control of a
hooked fish. Here the power of the rod is used to
keep a hooked bass from running into the weeds.*

Patience will win out and, besides, learning to cast is a pleasure once the rudimentary steps are learned. You can't go fishing every day, sometimes not even every week, but you can usually find time to *cast* a little every day. Your patience with bait-casting gear will be well rewarded; you will have mastered the basic equipment necessary for consistently good catches of bass.

Bait-Casting Rods

There is no such thing as the "ideal" bait-casting rod. Fishermen can choose longer rods with lighter actions so that the lightest weight lures can be cast a reasonable distance; they can also buy shorter rods with stiffer actions for fishing with heavier lines and larger lures. Individual preferences are so diverse that what is "ideal" to one guy will be unacceptable to the next. I can only offer you some guidelines in purchasing a rod and list some of my own preferences.

First, I like rods of one-piece construction. This means I'm using a single, continuous piece of fiberglass (or graphite, the latest but relatively expensive rod material) which stretches from inside the tiptop guide down to the offset reelseat. I feel the one-piecer provides the utmost in strength, since it has no joints susceptible to stress.

Older models of two-piece rods once had a tendency to break at the *ferrules*, the female-male connecting parts of the rod, when great stress was placed on the bending rod blanks. Ferrules were commonly made of metal, a nonflexing material compared to the more flexible rod. The rod would bend, but the ferrule would not, and whap!—another broken rod. There have been advances in ferrule construction, the best, in my opinion, being the glass-on-glass ferrule designed so that a tapering section of the rear fiberglass blank slips snugly *inside* the front half of the rod. Manufacturers claim that this, as a result, allows the entire rod to flex, eliminating the metal ferrule, yet providing a two-piece rod.

I own a couple of spinning rods with this ferrule design and must report I have had no breakage problem with either of them, after catching many fish.

Still, since I *know* there are no joining parts in my one-piece rods, I'm more confident in using them and applying pressure to hooked fish. Assuming a glass-on-glass ferrule does not weaken a rod, I *know* that my one-piece rods are, at worst, no weaker—and they may be stronger than a two-piece rod. Besides, I don't have to worry about the rod sections sticking together. I still find two-piece rods occasionally "mating," making me utter some fine four-letter syllables while I try to get them apart so they'll fit back into their two-piece-size rod case.

When I have used those two-piece spinning rods, I've always made sure they were snugly joined before making a cast, but I can't say the same for a few other fishermen I've watched. I suppose that carelessness adds a little more humor to our lives. At least, *I* think it's amusing when a beginner casts the top half of his rod 20 feet out into the lake and must then retrieve his line to reclaim a vital part of his equipment.

So, I like one-piece bait-casting rods. I also like two lengths: 5½- and 6-footers. If I had but one rod to fish with, I'd select a 5½-foot, medium-light-action, fast-taper blank. This selection could handle a range of 10- to 17-pound test lines and ⅜- to ¾-ounce lures, although it would be best suited for 12- to 15-pound test lines and ½- to ⅝-ounce lures. The rod is long enough to make reasonably long casts, yet short enough to handle comfortably. Its fast-taper design would include a tip section light enough to absorb the shock of a spurting fish or detect a light bite on live bait and a butt section strong enough to set the hook forcefully, especially when using plastic worms. For me, this is the combination I've settled on for the near-ideal rod. But notice I said *near*; it is still not *totally* ideal.

I normally take along two 5½-foot bait-casting rods when bass fishing, their only difference being that one is a medium-light action and the other is a medium action. The medium-light model is good for pitching crank-plugs, spinnerbaits, topwater lures, and plastic worms. The medium-class model, because of its slightly stiffer action, is used for working with the larger crankplugs, live bait (when large bass in thick brush are the quarry), or heavy leadhead jigs in deep water.

The third rod I include on trips is a 6-foot, medium-action bait-casting stick. Because of its 72-inch length, it will heave a lure just a mite farther than the 5½-footer. I find this is an advantage when long casts are necessary to hook spooky fish in shallow water. The 6-footer is used almost exclusively with plugs and will cover a lot of territory in a single cast.

My fourth selection is a 5½-foot graphite rod, a light-action staff manufactured by the Fenwick Tackle Company. This little beauty, far lighter and smaller in diameter than a conventional fiberglass rod of the same length and action, is a joy to use for light-tackle fishing. It easily handles 8- and 10-pound test lines and lures down to ¼ ounce and provides practically tireless casting throughout a full day on the water. One of the properties of graphite causes this rod to magnify the slightest tap on a plastic worm (or bottom structure of the lake), giving me the advantage of its highly sensitive "feel."

To see just how sensitive graphite rods are to "feel," try this little test. Hold a graphite rod in your hand, grasping it as you normally would around the reelseat. Close your eyes. Have your buddy *barely* scratch the tiptop with a fingernail. Surprisingly, you'll be able to clearly feel that scratching down at the handle, and you'll know exactly when he starts and stops the scratching. That's real sensitivity.

Other features to look for when purchasing a bait-casting rod are:
1. Hard-chromed or stainless steel guide frames, for long life.

2.   Ceramic guide inserts, which produce less friction as the line rubs against the guides during a cast, thereby increasing casting distance.

3.   Reel-locking mechanisms which hold the reel firmly to the reel-seat, yet have convenient tightening devices (some locking mechanisms are difficult to tighten down and untighten, and they allow the reel to wiggle on the reelseat.

4.   An offset reel handle design which fits comfortably in *your* hand (I have no preference for using straight handles over the newer, "pistol grip" handles, but it may make a difference to you).

5.   Rod guide windings which are *sufficiently* coated with protective resin, so that the windings will last several seasons before unraveling.

6.   A cushioned, rod butt cap, larger in diameter than the diameter of the rod butt itself. (I have a habit of sticking the rod butt against one side of my lower chest when fighting a fish and, after several fish, I get a sore spot there if the rod butt cap isn't cushioned well.)

Bait-Casting Reels

Since almost all of the major manufacturers offer good products, you have relatively little chance of mis-selecting a bait-casting reel. The Penn Reel Company, Garcia Corporation, Pflueger, and Daiwa all make adequate revolving spool reels for bass fishing. Garcia's Ambassadeur 5000 and 5500 series are probably the country's largest sellers and my own personal choice.

No matter which brand you select, I would recommend you buy a high-gear ratio, fast-retrieve reel. These cost a little more than the standard ratio reels, but they take a lot of wrist work out of retrieving or quickly taking up slack line before setting a hook when plastic worm fishing. While most standard-retrieve bait-casting reels operate on about a 3.5-to-1 ratio (for every one complete turn of the reel handle, the reel spool revolves three and one-half times), the fast-retrieve models approach nearly a 5-to-1 ratio. Garcia's Ambassadeur 5500 and 5500C, for example, have 4.7-to-1 retrieve ratios.

Look at it this way. A high-ratio reel retrieves more line per turn of the reel handle and, operating at the fastest speed you can produce (the speed at which you can wind the handle), is going to gain line faster than the standard retrieve. You can always *slow down* the retrieve of a fast-ratio reel to match fishing conditions, but you can't increase the speed of a standard-ratio reel beyond your physical limits.

Some of the larger ⅝- and ¾-ounce, deep-diving plugs *require* a fast-retrieve reel to produce the proper action and reach the proper depth of the plug design. Also, "buzzing" or "gurgling" a spinnerbait is much easier with a fast retrieve. Consider, too, that once you decide your lure has passed completely through a suspected bass hangout, often only the water in the end portion of your cast, then the faster you get that lure back to the boat, the sooner you can recast to a different spot. High-speed reels can save fishing time by allowing you to cover more water in a day, especially when fishing with "percentage" artificials such as spinnerbaits and crank-plugs. (We'll discuss these lures and their fishing methods in subsequent chapters.)

I prefer bait-casting reels with large reel handles and good-size, knurled fingerknobs, features not all makes of reels possess. A man has big hands, not easily adaptable to small handles, so I'd stay away from the dainty designs.

A quick-take-apart feature is an advantage, too, for changing reel spools quickly or servicing the reel. One of the most popular designs of quick-take-apart reels has three knurled screw knobs on the transmission side of the reel (the "fat" side containing the handle) that screw into the inner sideplate and support posts, holding the entire unit together. When these knobs are unscrewed, the reel comes apart in three basic sections: right sideplate (with handle), spool, and left sideplate (with reel support posts and reelseat).

When purchasing a quick-take-apart, look for knobs which have *slotted* heads so that a screwdriver may be used to tighten and loosen the take-apart screws; otherwise, the screws may back off by themselves. Few things feel as foolish as suddenly seeing the right side of your reel fall off into the boat . . . or the lake. The same is true for the nut which holds the handle on the reel: Look for a nut with a locking device which prevents the nut from loosening and backing off. Or else stock extra handles in your tackle box.

Spool capacity isn't as important in bass fishing as it is in some other forms of angling. In big-game ocean fishing, for instance, capacity requirements are in terms of multiple hundreds of yards of line, as the fish are very large and capable of swift, powerful runs. As the bass fisherman, however, normally works with only the first 50-odd yards of line on the spool, bait-casting reel spools often hold more line than necessary. Therefore you may prefer a reel which can be modified for the type of fishing that you're doing. For example, the Garcia Ambassadeur 5500C is rated for 190 yards of 15-pound test monofilament line, a fine combination for light saltwater fishing, but a potential waste of line for freshwater bassin'. To accommodate the latter, the reel comes equipped with a second spool arbor (a two-piece core) which can be snapped over the original arbor to *decrease* the line capacity, making it more practical for bass angling.

What's enough line? I think 100 yards is plenty, for any test line ranging from 8 to 20 pounds. Remember, as you increase the strength of the same brand of line, you are also increasing its diameter; hence, a reel holding 100 yards of 15-pound test will hold substantially more than that of 10-pound test.

If your bait-casting reel holds too much line for your fishing conditions and does not come with an optional, attachable spool arbor, you can use some form of backing on the reel spool, underneath the fishing line, to take up the space: adhesive tape, cotton string, dacron line, or any material which will build up evenly on the bottom of the spool.

Never wind a smaller amount of line directly on a much larger capacity spool without taking up the extra space with backing. Otherwise, the line won't fill the spool space properly—it won't come within the correct mark of ⅛ inch from the outer edge of the spool diameter—and casting will be difficult. *Short-filling* the spool (using no backing) will decrease casting distance and increase the tendency to backlash.

Most bait-casting reels utilize a star-drag mechanism for adjusting the friction against the revolving spool when the reel gears are engaged and, in turn, regulating the amount of "drag" the fish must overcome to pull line from the spool. Design changes through the years have produced much smoother operating and more dependable drag mechanisms on all major brand reels. I have, for example, enjoyed fine results and found no large differences in using Penn, Garcia, or Daiwa bait-casting reels.

The combination of a Fenwick "Lunker Stik" bait-casting rod and an Ambassadeur reel took this California limit of five largemouth bass.

I have one piece of advice on drags. Always back off (loosen) the star-drag adjustment when the reel is not in use to relieve the pressure on the inner drag washers and prevent the washers from sticking or freezing up when the reel is stored. The washers will then give better performance and wear longer.

Spinning Gear

Open-face spinning tackle is popular among many bass fishermen. A few of the big-name, professional tournament fishermen use open-face spinning equipment exclusively; far more, however, use spinning gear only as supplemental equipment.

Basically, spinning tackle is designed for lighter work, for use with lighter-pound test lines and smaller, lighter-weight lures. Because the open-face spinning reel uses a stationary spool design, there is almost no inertia to overcome while line uncoils, and because spinning rod actions are generally lighter than bait-casting rod actions (in layman's terms, the spinning rod is smaller in diameter and more limber or "whippier"), they will flex more easily and under less weight and will more effectively toss out the smaller artificials.

The single, greatest advantage I have found in using open-face spinning gear is that it works well in catching wary, spooky fish. After all, bass don't hit with reckless abandon all the time; sometimes conditions such as a high sun, ultraclear water, and shallow depths combine to make the quarry downright cautious. That's when fishing gets tough, and the terminal tackle must be scaled down to finesse the fish into striking.

Spinning tackle also works well in live-bait fishing. Its light-action rod design allows the slightest strike to be felt at the rod tip and allows a live bait to be softly lob-cast so that it won't snap off the hook in midair, as could happen with a stiffer-action rod. In addition, the bass feels less drag when he swims off with a live bait, because the line is *uncoiling* from a stationary reel spool, rather than being *pulled off* a revolving spool which creates some friction against the sides of the reel.

Spinning tackle, of course, can much more quickly be mastered by a complete beginner, who would otherwise need a great deal more time to learn the basics of bait-casting. Therein lies one beauty of spinning. Spin fishing *creates* fishermen, because in just a few minutes a novice can be taught to cast. The disadvantage to this ease in learning, however, is that many fishermen never advance to bait-casting gear. Maybe they don't have the confidence to attempt the revolving spool reel or they don't wish to invest the time to adapt to bait-casting, but whatever their reasons, a lot of anglers become fixated on the fixed-spool reel.

In my opinion, the versatile bass angler masters spinning as an alternative form of angling, but he is definitely limiting his ability to hook fish if he never progresses to bait-casting.

Spinning Rods

I've developed two favorites in spinning rods. One is used for live-bait fishing or for fishing crankplugs, spinnerbaits, or, occasionally, topwater lures; the other is used for very light, practically ultralight fishing, when bass are exceptionally spooky.

The longer of these two choices is a 6-foot, medium-light-action spinning rod designed to handle 8- to 12-pound test lines and ⅜- to ½-ounce lures or live bait. The rod, manufactured by the Quick Corporation of America, is of fast-taper design and has a specially designed Neo-grip reelseat which uses neoprene rubber to hold the reel to the rod. Since the reelseat contains no metal, this rod is a joy to use in cold weather. (If you've ever touched the metal parts of a rod or reel in cold weather, you know how "frozen" these can feel—and how quickly that bitter coldness goes through your fingers.)

I use a one-piece model manufactured by Fenwick for very difficult fishing conditions, when fish want the smallest of lures and lightest of lines. This 5-foot, fast-taper, light-action model handles 1/16- to 5/16-ounce lures and 4- to 6-pound test. As it is so light, making a small fish feel quite large, I also use it just for fun.

Here are some features to look for in purchasing a spinning rod: chromed or stainless-steel guide frames, ceramic guide inserts, secure reel-locking mechanisms (any fixed, metal reelseat rod should have double-locking screw rings), a comfortable handle and finger knob, a sufficient coating of finish to protect the rod guide windings for several seasons of use, one-piece construction, and a cushioned butt cap.

 Why?

Spinning Reels

Many fine open-face spinning reels are available on the market today. Among the more popular are those manufactured by the Garcia Corporation (the "Mitchell" series), Quick Corporation of America (the "Finessa" series), Daiwa, Pflueger, and Penn.

Perhaps describing the models I use would be a good way to point out features you should consider in purchasing a good, open-face spin reel.

The reel I use on my 6-foot, medium-light-action spin rod is a Garcia Mitchell 410, the high-speed version of the famous "300." This unit features a 4.8-to-1 gear ratio, two sets of roller bearings, a pushbutton spool which allows you to change spools in seconds, a Teflon drag system, a full bail with hard-chromed roller guide, and a one-spot lubrication system. The spool capacity is about 125 yards of 8-pound test line with an arbor added or 300-plus yards of 8-pound test without the addition of an arbor.

My lighter spin outfit takes a Quick Finessa 110, an 8-ounce reel with a 4.75-to-1 gear ratio, full bail, 200-yard capacity for 6-pound test, a tungsten carbide line guide, pushbutton spool release, fold-away handle, and has a handle-conversion feature which allows either right or left hand use, although I only use the customary lefthand handle mount.

Spinning reels will give years of service with a minimum of care. They should be oiled or lubed periodically as indicated in the owner's manual, and you should check occasionally to see that the line roller guide doesn't freeze up. The roller guide must revolve as line is drawn from the reel spool while the bail is closed; otherwise, a frozen roller may soon develop a groove and eventually fray the line. Always remember to back off the drag adjustment on a spinning reel, as on a bait-casting reel, when it is not in use as this will relieve the pressure on the inner drag washers and prevent them from sticking or prematurely wearing out.

Multiple Outfits

As I've said, there's really no *ideal* rod-and-reel combination for bass fishing. Fishing conditions on any given day can vary so much that serious bass fishermen may use several outfits, as evidenced by my owning the four bait-casting outfits and two spinning outfits which I've described above. When you increase your number of fishing outfits—to a reasonable degree, of course—you increase your versatility as a bass angler and therefore increase your chances of success.

Multiple fishing outfits also save a lot of time. Say, for instance, that an angler limits himself to only one rod-and-reel combination. If he wants to start off his day fishing with a plastic worm, he has to rig that lure on his line and then take the time to rerig when he wants to switch lures. By the time he cuts off the worm rig, locates his second choice in his tackle box, puts the worm rig back in the box, takes out the new choice, and ties it on his line, he has lost perhaps 4 or 5 minutes of fishing time. That may not seem like much, but multiply that by the number of times a fisherman may have to switch until he discovers what the bass prefer, and he's lost a substantial amount of time which he could have used for fishing. And the line *in the water* catches the fish.

On the other hand, say you have four outfits all rigged up at the beginning of the day. You could have a plastic worm on one rod and reel, a crankplug on another, a spinnerbait on a third, and a leadhead jig on the fourth. You can change outfits and lures in seconds and be pitching out a different offering in a fraction of the time it would take to rerig your one and only outfit.

Sometimes you happen on a school of passing fish which provide you with some fast action—but for only a few, short moments. Then your success becomes a function of the number of casts you can make and the number of fish you can get to the boat in a limited amount of time. If you have only a single outfit and you snag your lure on the second cast, that school of fish could well be gone by the time you tie on another lure. It's far better to be able to simply pick up a second, prerigged outfit and keep on fishing.

Fishing line

There are a few variations possible, but the majority of today's Western bass fishermen use monofilament line in their angling.

Major manufacturers have made great improvements in "mono" in the past decade, and they now produce lines which are far smaller in diameter (per pound-test strength) than was ever before possible. Today's name-brand monofilament also has good abrasion-resistance, controlled stretch, easy knot-tying characteristics, low visibility in the water, good limpness, and improved shock resistance.

But all of these advances haven't taken the risk out of buying mono-filament—unless you buy a name brand. Practically nowhere else in tackle selection is buying a quality product more important. *Remember, the line is the only link between the fish and the fisherman.*

It is far more probable that a fish can be landed on quality line and a mediocre rod-and-reel outfit than on mediocre line and a fine quality rod-and-reel combo. Insist on high-grade line. Consider brands such as Maxima, Stren, Cortland, Berkely, and others made by the large tackle firms, and then buy the *highest grade* line they offer.

Heat is an enemy of monofilament. Never store spools of nylon line or reels filled with line in a hot place because the heat will adversely affect its chemical composition and shorten its useful life. To protect line against heat, I wrap small sheets of aluminum foil around the spools which I keep in my garage.

When you're filling your reel, keep a slight tension on the line so the monofilament will pack evenly on the spool and come off uniformly later when you're casting. A loosely laid line will cause backlashes. (A dry line will tend to backlash, too, so never attempt a long distance cast until after you've made a few shorter ones to get the line thoroughly wet.)

One of the chief causes of lost fish is old, worn-out line, which some fishermen neglect to replace. Just how frequently you should replace line depends on the type of fishing you do and how often you go fishing. Line which sees much use around brush, rocks, and other line-fraying structure should be replaced more often than line used in more open water. (The former is usually the case in bass fishing.) Fishing more often means replacing line more often. Would you believe some professional tournament fishermen, competing in the largest cash-award events, change their line *every day*? It's true.

While individual cases will vary, here is a guide for line replacement frequency:

1. *Occasional fishing* (only three to six times a year): change at least once a year;

2. *Frequent fishing* (two or three times a month): change at least three times a year.

3. *Very frequent fishing* (four to eight times a month): change four or five times a year.

4. *Expert or professional fishing* (with the frequency of a professional, tournament fisherman or fishing guide): change a minimum of once a month, possibly more frequently.

The greatest wear normally occurs in the last 3 or 4 feet of line when you're fishing, so a good angler continually checks this portion of the line for nicks and frays. This section continually rubs back and forth through the rod tip during casting and is also the section most likely to snag when a lure or bait hangs up. It's good practice to routinely cut off this section two or three times during a day to ensure you have the best possible line working for you.

When you check your line for frays, rely on your fingers more than your eyes. A badly frayed spot along the line can usually be *seen*, but lesser-frayed areas often must be detected by *feel*; slowly run your thumb and forefinger together along the line to discover those abrasions that are missed by your eyes.

Most good knots will provide 95 to 100 percent of the original line strength after they are tied, but a sloppily tied knot can weaken a line as much as 50 percent. Never use a questionably tied knot; it isn't worth the risk of losing a good fish. If in doubt, take a few seconds to cut your line and carefully retie a knot which you know is correct.

Tackle Boxes

A tackle box is a container to carry your bass fishing gear. There are two main considerations in selecting a box: (1) the box should be roomy enough to hold all your gear and (2) it should hold that gear in an *organized and readily accessible manner*. Almost all of the medium- and higher-priced boxes today are of strong construction, are corrosion resistant, have ABS plastic trays (which means plastic worms will no longer "melt" the trays), and have good latches and comfortable handles. Just be certain your box allows you to readily locate lures, hooks, sinkers, and other tackle. It's very frustrating to reach for a preferred lure at a critical moment, when the fish are biting, and instead find a tangled mess in that tray compartment because too many items are crammed into too little space.

In the past half a dozen years, several boxes made especially for the bass angler have emerged on the market. These smaller specialty boxes are often designed to accommodate a certain type of lure, so a serious basser may carry along a plastic worm box, a spinnerbait box, a crankplug box, or a combination of boxes. The value of these boxes, some with transparent plastic lids, is that they hold a tremendous number of lures in a relatively small space. Three or four of these smaller units will hold many times more gear than one very large, all-purpose box. Since they are smaller, they can be placed right at your feet for instant use. I regularly use a couple of specialized boxes—a Rebel Series 800 Excalibur and a Rebel BB-50 Bass 'N Box—and together they place a veritable tackle store at my finger-tips.

Accessory Gear

I will discuss lures, hooks, and sinkers in later chapters, but I want to list here some other items I like to take along on bass fishing expeditions:

1. A small scale, so I'm not tempted to become too much of a liar. ←

2. A large landing net with at least an 18-inch diameter and a 36-inch handle, so it will accommodate the *biggest* fish I can expect to catch. ←

3. A pair of diagonal cutters for cutting line. (Some people like to use fingernail clippers.) *O.H.*

4. A pair of "fisherman's pliers" for removing hooks and clamping on splitshot. ←

5. A pair of conventional pliers and a screwdriver for general repairs.

6. A reel tool, a small reel repair kit, and a tube of lubricant (comes with most better-grade bait-casting reels). *Get these.*

7. Compact rain gear. *O.H.*

8. A small can of aerosol lubricant (WD-40 or LPS is good). *O.H.*

9. A small sharpening stone for retouching hook points. *O.H.*

10. A folding knife. *O.H.*

11. Two stainless steel fish stringers of the type which are plastic covered and come with a snap-swivel at each clip; these stringers cost $5 to $7.50 each, but are well worth the money for their strength and durability. *Why two?*

12. A piece of toweling for wiping hands when live-bait fishing. *O.H.*

13. A pair of sunglasses. *O.H.*

14. Suntan lotion or Chapstick, depending on weather conditions. ←

15. A visored cap for sun protection. ←

16. A camera and film. *Forget it, unless you're a writer.*

2

The Bass Fishing Machine

Any list of inventions which have greatly changed the sport of bass fishing should certainly include the modern-day bass boat.

I can still recall my first experience fishing in this type of craft. Previously, my bass fishing had been confined to the standard, runabout boat or, at best, to those then-speedy, little aluminum models, like the Gregor which many lake rental fleets contained. No more than a dozen years ago, a sturdy, little 14-foot Gregor and a 20-horsepower motor was considered by many bass anglers to be an ideal combination.

One day my phone rang, and a good friend invited me to go bass fishing in his "new rig." It was a 16-foot Astroglas. A bass boat. I was more than mildly impressed when I first saw the gleaming, metal-flake finish of his new acquisition—a touch of glamour previously reserved for "hot dog" ski boats. The bass boat had classy lines: It was low slung, had a nicely flared bow and a racy trihedral hull design, plus full interior carpeting and beautifully upholstered seats. But, I asked myself, would this piece of molded fiberglass really help a bass angler catch more bass?

I suspected the answer after only a single day of fishing, and have become even more thoroughly convinced through the years—a resounding YES!

I was surprised, at the end of that first day of bass-boat fishing, to discover my posterior had taken so well to those upholstered, swiveling casting seats, and I felt no soreness or tiredness. Fishing was a pleasure without the constant shuffling that seemed to occur on the bench seats of the more primitive rental boats or the aluminum models. Also, because of the elevation the bass-boat seats provided, we could cast farther and more accurately.

The speed at which we covered the distances between fishing spots saved a lot of valuable fishing time. Instead of poking along, we would zip from spot to spot in a matter of minutes, although the lake we were fishing

These fishermen work a rocky shoreline in search of bass.
Their boat provides them with speed, comfort and a quiet
trolling motor and elevated casting seats.

was nearly 5 miles long. I know the time saved by our swift speed at least *doubled* the amount of casts we could make which doubled our chances of catching fish.

The bow-mounted electric motor held us steady in an afternoon breeze which would have made fishing (or catching) much more difficult by drifting us too fast if we had been in a boat without such a device or in a boat with a stern-mounted electric motor, which would have caused much more bow swing.

In short, we caught a lot of bass that day, and I attribute a significant part of our catch to the style of boat I was aboard.

Few fishermen today would debate whether a bass boat gives an angler an edge in his pursuit of the largemouth bass. It does. A guy only has to decide whether he is serious enough about bass fishing to spend the $5,000 to $8,500 currently necessary to outfit his rig, including the costs of boat, motor, trailer, and accessories. And whether he can find a way to explain to his wife that he needs this fishing combination more than Johnny needs new braces on his teeth.

More than just a boat, this specially designed craft is a veritable fishing machine, a floating base of operations which offers its occupants several advantages over those in more conventional types of boats. Let's take a look at a hypothetical bass boat—one which is outfitted with a composite of equipment options—to see what makes a well-appointed bass boat practically as valuable as a rod and reel. Here's what we'd probably find:

A craft 17 to 19 feet long, large enough to ride and fish well in most choppy water, yet small enough to handle and maneuver easily in tight quarters. On the largest lakes of the West, especially those of the Colorado River chain (Powell, Mead, Mohave, and Havasu), bass boats in the 19- to 21-foot class may offer better protection from rough weather.

A boat with a relatively shallow draft, providing it with good speed and making it very adaptable to shallow water.

Both front and rear, swivel-type, pedestal seats, each mounted on an elevated casting platform, thus providing excellent visibility, lure control, and a wide range of fishing territory. The movement of the seats allows a fisherman to change the direction of his casting by simply swiveling around with his feet on the deck. This is much less tiring than shifting most of the body on a hard bench which really only faces fore and aft.

Bow and stern, remote anchoring systems, allowing both fore and aft anchors to be lowered and retrieved by controls located on or near the driver's console. Two anchors, instead of one, hold the boat steadier in a breeze. The centrally located controls save effort and time.

A bow-mounted, electric trolling motor with foot-operated controls, allowing the bow-seat angler to change speed or direction of the boat while leaving his hands free to fish. The trolling motor also provides near-noiseless propulsion in shallow water where fish may be spooked by the commotion of a large outboard motor.

Two livewells, each served by a water-circulation pump, to keep the catch alive so the fish can be released later after photos or after a tournament weigh-in. If the fish are to be eaten, the livewell keeps the catch fresher for the table.

Swift cruising capability from spot to spot, made possible by a high-powered, power-tilt outboard motor. Most commonly, bass-boat power-plants now range from 75 to 150 horsepower, although some smaller and some larger are in use.

Two electronic depthfinders, one mounted on the bow of the boat where the bow-seat fisherman can receive a continuous bottom structure readout while he's fishing and the other mounted on the driver's console where the driver (or stern-seat fisherman) can check the depth and bottom contour from his station.

Large storage lockers to hold fishing gear, lunches, jackets, personal floatation devices, cameras, line, the spare prop, rain gear, and the many other items which find their way aboard fishing boats.

Fishing rod racks which hold rigged rods and reels securely, yet leave them accessible for immediate use.

The list of extras seems to be limited only by the imagination of manufacturers or the income of anglers, for, in addition to the above, some fishermen also outfit their bass boats with bow-mounted, tilt-control switches, so the outboard lower unit can be raised to clear shallow spots while the angler remains in the bowseat; CB radios for contacting "buddy" boats to obtain on-the-water fishing information; combination water-temperature gauges and oxygen meters; graph recorders which not only indicate the depth but offer a continuous printout of bottom structure on graph paper; or even stereo tape systems (please don't play hard rock when I am fishing within a mile of you).

Just what options are the most necessary and which are more expendable? It's a matter of personal choice; *I* would say a *basic* bass-boat rig

WBFA official Bill Rice flips out a cast from the front of this bass boat. Behind him is Wayne Cummings, another well-known Western bass angler.

*A fleet of modern bass boats are tied to the dock
as fog shrouds the water just before the beginning of
a major fishing tournament.*

should contain at least a bow-mounted trolling motor with footswitch, one
depthfinder mounted on the console, a moderate-size outboard (the largest
outboards are fast and can quickly empty a pocketbook) of 80 to 125 horsepower, an aeration system for the livewells, a bilge pump, U.S. Coast
Guard–approved PFDs (personal floatation devices), a fire extinguisher,
an emergency signalling device, running lights, a spotlight, a tachometer,
a water-pressure gauge (to check the outboard's water pump), an amp-
meter, plus any other safety devices which may be required by the Coast
Guard for the size of craft you purchase.

For what it's worth—and it could be worth your life—I'll say that high-
powered bass boats don't scare me, but a few bass boat *operators* have
made me take a deep breath or two. Hang a 150- to 200-horsepower outboard on a sleek, low-slung hull and you have a potential speed of 60 or
more miles per hour on flat water, given some of the high-performance
craft now on the market. And that's faster than we're legally allowed to
drive on freeways, at least as this book was being written.

Because of the torque created by these high-powered outboards, the
steering linkage systems of bass boats must withstand a great strain. It

makes little sense to me to find out just what the breaking point is by hot-dogging at the wheel. Actually, as long as a person doesn't exceed the BIA (Boating Industry Association) recommended-horsepower rating for a particular boat and uses that boat-and-motor combo in a reasonable manner, he is probably far safer than he would be driving on the street.

But one foolish mistake in a missile on water could cause irreversible damage. In the early '70s there was, in fact, a minor rash of fatal bass-boat accidents until word got around among fishermen. Most of the victims were lacerated so badly by outboard props that they died before reaching a hospital. The main cause of accidents were: (1) *overpowering* a particular hull, so that the steering linkage eventually tore loose, flipping the boat at high speed, throwing its occupants into the water, and then running over them; and (2) *running at high speed*, striking a floating or underwater object, and flipping the boat, with the same tragic result.

The trend toward larger motors has led to the kill switch, an electrical device which plugs into the ignition system and is attached to the fisherman by a cord or lanyard. Think of it as a unit shaped like an auto cigarette lighter, which must be in its socket to stay "hot." When he is operating the outboard, the boat driver fastens the end of the cord to the life jacket he is wearing or another solid part of his clothing. Should the fast-moving boat strike an object in the water and throw the driver overboard, the plug is yanked from the ignition system and the motor shuts off so that the boat can't circle and kill somebody. I'd certainly recommend a kill switch for any bass-boat rig which is capable of tossing somebody into the water. It's an investment in your own safety.

I've known some bass anglers who joined the speed race when they first purchased their rigs but, after a few close calls, settled down. Don't misunderstand me, there is nothing wrong with using a high-powered rig to its safe potential; the danger is only in *abusing* it. If you abuse it with too-tight turns at high speeds, careless running over unfamiliar parts of a lake, or flying in the fog, it could cost you an arm and a leg. Literally. Or worse, your life.

So don't overpower your craft, and do operate it safely. After all, you've got to stay in one piece to make the payments on that thing.

3

The Art of Artificials

The largemouth bass is a pushover for lures.

That is compared to many other types of fish, this species is caught in large numbers on artificial lures. There is something inherently satisfying about fooling a fish into striking a whatsit made of molded plastic, wire struts, revolving blades, wiggly skirts, or a polished chunk of metal, and it's his fondness for hardware, I think, which makes the bass a favorite among fishermen.

At first glance, however, a confusing variety of lures seems available— each type with a wide range of sizes, colors, patterns, and weights. There are so many choices, in fact, that an entire book could be devoted to today's array of lures which, considering market research techniques, are often designed as much to catch *fishermen* as they are to catch *fish*.

Although offered in thousands of variations, the kinds of lures most commonly used to catch Western bass can be divided into six basic types: (1) soft lures (plastic worms and their many offshoots), (2) spinnerbaits, (3) leadhead jigs, (4) casting and jigging spoons, (5) crankplugs (shallow-, medium-, and deep-divers), and (6) topwater lures.

Each of these types requires generally different fishing techniques, often appropriate under different fishing conditions. You don't, for example, retrieve a topwater lure in the same manner (a technique) as a crankplug; you wouldn't use a shallow-running crankplug when the bass are located in 40 feet of water (a condition), as there a leadhead jig would be much more effective.

In most cases, you try to match the lure selection to the depth you are fishing and to your idea of the preference of the fish at that depth. Then you match the proper retrieve technique to the lure you select.

Soft Lures

So-called soft lures are those molded of soft, flexible plastic and include the popular plastic worm and its many derivations, such as plastic lizards, water snakes, waterdogs, and grubs. These lures are usually purchased unrigged, in multiple quantities, in packs of 3 to 6 or more, and are rigged by the angler before fishing.

Soft lures are different from most other bass lures in that *the soft lures have no built-in action of their own*. Therefore, the angler must create any action of the lure. This takes patience, which eventually leads to experience, which, in turn, leads to skill. Too many fishermen try soft lures for an hour or so and then give up because they don't catch any fish. Often their failure lies in not realizing that many of these lures must be worked s-l-o-w-l-y over the bottom, *teased* along to entice a strike, and that the fisherman must develop a sixth sense to "read" his line and detect a bite.

The various forms of soft lures can be fished in depths of only a few feet to 40 or 50 feet. When fishing soft lures in shallow water, from a couple of feet down to 6 feet, you should use the smaller sizes of these lures with lighter sinkers and 6- to 10-pound test line. My experience has been that many bass fishermen use soft-type artificials in water ranging from 6 to 25 feet and use other types of artificials for shallower or deeper water.

Plastic worms are, by far, the most popular of the soft lures. If you're accustomed to *actively* retrieving a lure, fishing "the worm" can be exasperating—at least, at first. Crankplugs and spinnerbaits can be zipped through the water; topwater lures can be splashed, gurgled, and popped; and spoons are jigged up and down; but the worm, like most other soft lures, must be retrieved delicately and slowly.

Plastic worms commonly range in length from 4 to 7½ or 8 inches, although a few ultralight variations are shorter and a few so-called hog bass worms are longer. Personally, and I know a lot of good bass anglers who would agree, I prefer the 6-inch worm. This seems to be long enough to discourage a lot of throw-back-size bass from hitting, yet short enough for a decent-size fish to vacuum the lure into its mouth. Still, the 4-inch and 7½-inch worms shouldn't be neglected; there are days when a shorter or longer offering is just different enough to get more strikes.

Pick any hue of the rainbow and you can purchase plastic worms in that color, as well as in banded, striped, spotted, and mottled designs. Some fishermen believe the darker worms work best in off-color water or on dark days, while the lighter ones are most effective in clear water or on bright days. I've seen enough exceptions, however, to suspect that bass can independently vary their color preferences from day to day. I have, for example, taken bass on purple plastic worms, from the same lake and on the same day that others did equally well with lime- or tan-colored worms.

Probably more bass are taken on purple or black worms than any other colors, but this could be due to purple and black patterns being the most popular at the cash register. More lures in these colors creep through the water, and the bass can't hit a color they aren't offered. Certain colors appear to be more effective on a lake-to-lake basis, too. Black worms, for instance, are highly effective in the San Diego chain of lunker lakes in Southern California, while cherry red and bright blue plastic 'crawlers work well at Lake Powell in Utah. As a result, the veteran bass angler carries a variety of colors and then switches his offering periodically until he discovers which color the fish want at that time.

During the first years of the plastic worm boom, the lure remained relatively standardized in shape, but recently, in the past half a dozen years, the worm has turned (pardon the pun) and mutated into such variations as curly-tail worms, twister-tail worms, split-tail worms, worms with ringed segments, worms with "air-chamber" lobes, and many more.

Every time an innovation hits the market, catches on that particular type of worm seem to upsurge, then to taper off. Why? This could be caused by two factors: (1) the introduction of the "new" worm is tied to advertising, which spurs sales of the "hot" new lures, resulting in a lot of fishermen tossing the thing into the water; and (2) bass which receive a lot of fishing pressure may become so conditioned to seeing the "old" plastic worms that, when a different twist does come by, they hit it simply because it's new.

In short, *all* of the worms (and other lures) will catch bass at one time or another, depending on sets of conditions which fishermen probably never will fully understand, but which involve such factors as fishing pressure, newness of the lure, skill of the individual fisherman, color, depth, light volume, individual lake, time of year, aggressiveness of individual fish, and on and on.

It's interesting to note that while these lures are called plastic *worms*, few lakes really contain worms that length. A 6-inch-long worm isn't normally found bouncing along in the waters of a lake; those found in a minority of lakes are usually buried in the mud. Consider, also, that though nightcrawlers are land creatures, they are extremely effective as live bait. What, then, accounts for bass striking a plastic worm? It certainly doesn't resemble a natural inhabitant like a crawfish or a shad. Take your pick of explanations: Maybe the bass are curious or aggressive, or perhaps, as one school of thought maintains, the plastic worms resemble small water snakes.

During the plastic worm boom of the 1960s, a lot of different rigging techniques were introduced, tested, and discarded. These methods ranged from sticking a hook crosswise through the middle of the worm, with almost the entire hook exposed, to burying the entire shank of the hook into the body of the worm, leaving only the bend and point of the hook exposed. Finally, many bass fishermen settled on one procedure—the

"Texas-style" rigging—which combines simplicity, good fish-hooking capability, and snag-free performance.

To rig a plastic worm Texas-style, refer to the drawings on page 46 and follow these instructions:

1.   Thread a cone-shaped slip sinker (a sliding sinker with a hole through its center) on your line, with the pointed end of the sinker *facing up the line* toward the rod.

2.   Tie on a plastic-worm–style hook (several styles are available; I've had good luck with straight shank, elbow shank, and curved shank hooks, but prefer the curved above all).

3.   Push the hook point into the center of the head of the worm (Figure 1).

4.   Bring the hook point into the center of the head of the worm (Figure 2), so that the point protrudes about ¼ to ½ inch below the head of the worm.

5.   Pull the hook through the worm and out the side hole until the eye of the hook only remains embedded in about ¼ inch of the worm.

6.   Turn the hook (Figure 3) so that the barb faces the worm. Gently push the worm forward with one hand, holding the head securely against the eye of the hook with the other hand, and then reinsert the hook point into the worm until the point almost comes out the opposite side of the worm.

7.   When the worm is properly rigged (Figure 4), it will hang straight on the line. If you do not slightly bunch up the worm before reinserting the hook point, the worm will be too curved to appear lifelike.

Plastic waterdogs, lizards, and small water snakes can all be rigged in the same manner. The small plastic grubs, however, are usually rigged on a molded, lead jig head. The hook of the jig head is inserted into the middle of the plastic grub head, and the grub is threaded onto the shank of the hook until the grub head is about ⅜ inch from the back of the lead head. Then the hook point is brought out of the grub so that the point, barb, and most of the bend of the hook are exposed before the grub is pushed the rest of the way up behind the head of the jig.

Most bass fishermen use 3/16- to 5/8-ounce slip sinkers with their plastic worms, choosing the lighter weights in that range for shallow water, the heavier weights for deeper water. Grubs commonly range from ¼ to ½ ounce. The most commonly used worm hooks are sizes 2/0 and 3/0.

Now that we've got our soft lure rigged, how do we retrieve it? Plastic 'crawlers, salamanders, lizards, and water snakes are usually most effective when fished slowly. Here's how:

1.   Begin by making a cast to your target (may be a visible target above the surface or "blind" water when you're working an underwater structure).

2.   Allow the plastic worm or other soft lure to sink slowly to the

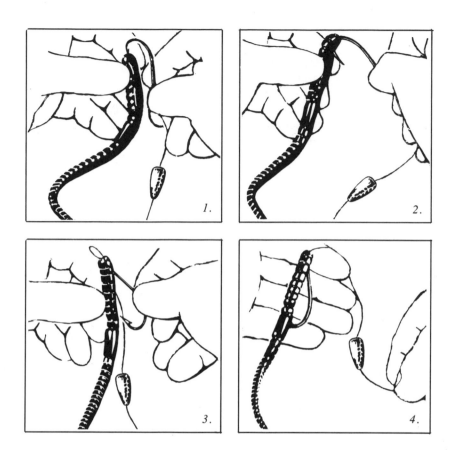

bottom, but always be alert for a strike—seen or felt as a sudden twitch or "jump" of the line—as the worm is sinking.

3.   Lower the rod to a 10 o'clock position and quickly take up slack line.

4.   S-L-O-W-L-Y twitch the rod tip up to a 12 o'clock position, pausing for a second or two between each three or four slight twitches. One series of twitches, from 10 to 12 o'clock, may take 15 to 20 seconds. These twitches transfer down the line and cause the worm to hop or bounce along, rising just an inch or so off the bottom with each twitch and then resettling to the bottom.

The idea is to make the worm appear so enticing, tantalizing, and irresistible in its slow, crawling movement that a bass just can't pass it up. You can practice these twitches in clear, shallow water to see what effect they have on the lure. Most strikes occur not on the *pull* part of the twitch but as the worm is falling back down.

5.   After the rod reaches a 12 o'clock position, pause a second for any late biters, then drop the rod tip back to 10 o'clock, take up slack, and repeat the process.

The slow twitching of the worm, through the 10 to 12 o'clock positions, should be kept up as long as you feel the worm is still in good bass territory. Sometimes that covers only the first few feet the worm travels through the water; at other times it covers the distance all the way back to the boat.

When a bass strikes a plastic worm, the sensation sent up to the rod tip can vary from a forceful jolt which feels as if the fish hooked itself to a twitch so nearly imperceptible you'll want to set the hook on suspicion. Generally, however, the strike comes as a gentle tap-tap-tap which can be both seen (always *watch* your line for twitches) and felt (feel can be improved by holding the line between a thumb and forefinger, just in front of the reel, as you are making the upward twitches of the rod tip).

Learning to tell the difference between a bass strike and the lure merely running over rocks and brush is largely a matter of experience. Obviously, that difference is difficult to explain on paper; I can point out that a rock and brush "strike" usually occurs on the *pull*, not the fall of the lure, and rocks and brush feel much more *solid* than the smallish tap of a bass. Again, practice in clear, shallow water and, when you see the worm crawling through brush or rocks, close your eyes and feel that sensation through the rod tip and the line. You'll soon learn, in this shallow-water classroom, to tell the difference between bottom structure and bass.

When you do feel a bass bite, you've got to act fast, because once that soft lure is in the fish's mouth, chances are it won't stay there nearly as long as if it were live bait. The slow twitching of the lure makes the bass strike, but there's little attraction in that plastic to make him want to hang on. When you feel the first strike, immediately drop the rod tip to a 9 o'clock position parallel to the surface of the water, simultaneously taking the slack out of the line (you'll create slack by dropping the tip), and *the instant the line comes tight with the rod at 9 o'clock, strike up with the rod tip as if you're trying to tear the fish's head off.* The steps, again: (1) strike of fish, (2) drop rod and take up slack, and (3) set the hook with force.

I once heard a big-name pro angler giving advice to a large audience at a bass seminar and, in answer to a question about plastic worm fishing, he said, "I try to set the hook a split-second *before* the bass sucks in the plastic worm."

It would be impossible, of course, to know when a bass was going to strike, but his point was well taken: The hook must be set *as soon as possible* following the strike. There're just too many bass which spit a worm only a second or two after they inhale it.

There are two reasons for setting the hook *hard.*

First, as the hook point is still inside the plastic worm even though *almost* breaking through, it's necessary to set the hook with sufficient force to drive the point through the worm and into the fish. Not only must the

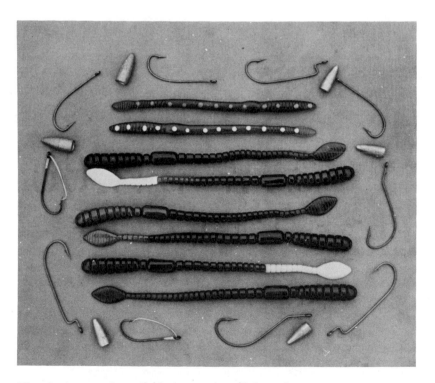

The plastic worm is available in a variety of sizes, shapes, textures, and patterns. Also shown here are the cone-shaped "worm" sinkers and an assortment of "worm" hooks.

barb stick into the bass, but also enough of the bend of the hook (about ⅛ inch) so that the barb will remain in the fish.

Second, striking hard may disorient a bass during those first critical seconds when it is hooked and, if it's a good fish, you can often get it turned and coming a few feet your way before it realizes what happened. If there're snags around, those few feet can mean the difference between a dandy catch and another one-that-got-away story.

Basically, the only difference between fishing a plastic worm and the larger soft lures such as imitation waterdogs and lizards is that the larger lures can be twitched along the bottom with *slightly* faster motion, using *slightly* longer hops.

Grubs can be fished with the twitch-and-hop retrieve, or in some instances they will draw strikes on a straight retrieve, still generally slow and bumping bottom. At yet other times, the grub works well when fished on long pulls of the rod tip which allow it to settle back down to the bottom between each pull.

I once watched a master of grub fishing, Bill Dance, scoop up nearly every bass in Southern California's Irvine Lake—or so it seemed that day —by artfully articulating a lime-colored grub. Bill, one of the all-time money winners of the Bass Anglers Sportsman Society, spent the better part of the day flicking his rod tip up to dance the grub, holding it steady as the grub was sinking, or keeping it bent as another bass grabbed the fraud. He was an accomplished soft lure fisherman, and it made those bass a soft touch.

Spinnerbaits

It's no surprise that the bait with the bladed spinners has become one of the most effective lures now cast into the kingdom of the bass. Spinner-baits are effective, versatile, and relatively easy to use. In a short time and with a little patience, an average angler can become a good one; an already good angler can emerge as a grave threat to the health of any bass.

Spinnerbaits aren't new. Ask a veteran of the bass wars and he'll tell you that old-school spinnerbait men used the Shannon double-spinner or one of the Arbogast Hawaiian Wigglers. Still relatively new, however, is the manufacture of the multiscore spinnerbaits and use of the innovative fishing methods which are now making bass take a second look at this lure.

A spinnerbait looks like nothing native to our bass fishing waters; at least, I don't think so. A spinnerbait has five basic parts: (1) a fore-mounted lead head, designed to provide casting weight and to make the bait sink; (2) a single or double wire strut which protrudes backward from the head of the lure at about a 45-degree angle; (3) one to three spinner blades suspended from a single-strut model or one or two blades fastened to each wire strut of a double-strut model; (4) an upright, single hook molded into the head of the lure; and (5) a vinyl or rubber skirt section, behind the head, partially covering the hook.

There we have it—like nothing Nature ever intended.

One characteristic of spinnerbait fishing is that bass will frequently strike the lure as it is sinking. Often this strike is so light the signal simply dies of exhaustion, short of reaching the rod tip. Learning to *watch* for that telltale twitch along the line is critical. When I was learning to fish these baits, I was outfished about 5-to-1 by a friend whom I swore had a sixth sense. He had the feel. Prepared for jolting strikes, I hadn't tuned down my senses to the fine adjustment necessary to perceive the tiny taps of the bass as the lure was sinking. My buddy, a skilled angler, watched for the slightest trace of a bite to be telegraphed up his monofilament. Every time he struck, something pulled back at the other end of the line.

Remember this: After you've made a cast and the lure is sinking, hold the rod at about a 45-degree angle—high enough to cause a *slight* slack or belly in the line to allow the bait to settle naturally, yet low enough to provide good leverage to strike if the line suddenly jumps or hops during its fall. Sure, some bass will wallop the lure so viciously they'll wind up committing suicide on the hook, but most will strike lightly.

There are roughly half a dozen techniques I know of and use to catch bass on spinnerbaits. Be innovative and experiment until you discover which methods work best for you.

When bass are in the shallows—say, from about 1 to 6 feet deep—the spinnerbait can be used much the same as a noisy surface lure.

One method is called *gurgling*. Bass gravitate toward cover in the shallows, so most surface spinnerbait fishing consists of casting to targets of visible cover—a tree, stump, brush pile, fence row, lily-pad bed, rocks, and other cover. Shallow-water cover immediately adjacent to areas of deep water are especially inviting to bass. Pitch the spinnerbait slightly *beyond* the target (4 to 6 feet), put the reel in gear, and begin your retrieve a split-second *before* the bait hits the water. The lighter, ¼- to ⅜-ounce spinnerbaits work best for this method.

Now, by using a rapid retrieve and holding the rod tip almost straight up until the bait is riding high, you can make the lure gurgle across the surface, beating its blades on the water and creating a splashing, churning trail which any bass can follow.

Another shallow-water technique is *buzzing*. To buzz a spinnerbait, slow down slightly from the speed used to gurgle the lure, but still retrieving at a relatively rapid speed. Now the blades of the bait will run just *below* the surface, creating a V-wake in the water.

Both gurgling and buzzing are good techniques to try in the spring and fall months, when the fish move up into shallow water areas.

The *target flutter* retrieve works in both shallow and mid-depth water, down to about 12 or 15 feet. Cast past your target, begin the retrieve instantaneously as the lure splashes down, and buzz the bait up to the target. Then make the bait "die"—that is, immediately stop the retrieve and let the lure flutter or drop beside the target. The sinking movement of the lure will slowly flutter the blades, and that unnerves a lot of bass.

One of my favorite methods of catching spinnerbait bass in the spring and early summer, in depths of 12 to 25 feet, is the *pick-up-and-sink* tech- (4) nique. I usually use a ½-ounce spinnerbait. This method is especially good when you are working moderate- to deep-sloping points, cliffs, bluffs, and bottom depressions.

The bait, once again, attracts with its fluttering blades. Cast to shallow water and work the bait out to deep water. After the lure sinks to the bottom, pick it up with a sharp flick of the rod tip, at the same time feeling for the vibration of the spinners up the line to tell you the bait is working properly. The snap must be not long but crisp enough to rattle the blades while raising the lure no more than 2 feet off the bottom. Let the bait flutter back down after each flick. Take in slack after each fall and watch for a strike while the bait is sinking.   (5)

One of the most unorthodox methods of working a spinnerbait is crawl- ing it slowly along the bottom, much the same as retrieving a plastic worm. I remember one trip when I was working a spinnerbait with the pick-up- and-sink method, my back turned to my fishing partner. He hooked three bass, brought each one to the boat with little commotion, and bounced them over the side. Each time, I only heard the fish flopping in the live- well, after he had already made another cast and flipped his artificial into the water. I watched the slow twitches of his rod tip as he gently nudged the lure along the bottom, working the rod from the 10 o'clock to 12 o'clock positions. I just figured he was casting a plastic 'crawler. And then I saw what he was using. He was creeping and pausing a light spinner- bait—at plastic worm speed—and knocking the beejeebers out of the bass.

Another way to use spinnerbaits is a form of *tule-dipping*. You just (6) move along and drop the lure straight down into pockets in heavy cover, letting the blades flutter and watching for a strike on the sink. If a strike doesn't happen while the lure is falling, try lifting the spinnerbait a few inches off the bottom and jigging it up and down. If there's still no action, move to the next pocket of cover.

The final way I occasionally fish a spinnerbait requires little finesse; (7) you cast it out and bring it back on a steady retrieve. It's a simple way to fish, but often very effective. Vary the depth you fish by the speed of the retrieve; wind slowly and it will run deeper, or faster and it will run more shallow.

One advantage of the spinnerbait is its ability to avoid snags. Because of the angle of the wire strut(s) above the hook and the function of the revolving blades in fending off hangups, a fisherman can pitch this lure into some very thick cover. Even if hung occasionally in overhanging brush, the spinnerbait can usually be freed if the angler pulls *slowly* on the line until the bait is almost up to the branch the line is draped across and then gives a gentle, quick flip of the rod to jump the lure over the branch.

There are no rigid rules covering the selection of colors, weights, and number of blades for spinnerbaits, but there are some helpful guidelines.

First, heavier spinnerbaits (up to ¾ ounce) are usually most effective in deep water; lighter models are better for shallow water.

Second, in murky, off-color water, go for more flash and brighter color in your spinnerbait selections. In water of average clarity, use an intermediate amount of flash and color. In ultraclear water, use less flash and the lighter hues.

How do you increase or decrease flash? Consider these effects: a *bigger* blade produces more flash than a smaller one of the same color and finish; a hammered-finish blade radiates more flash than a smooth-finish blade; a brass- or gold-finished blade gives off more flash than a silver; and, all other features being the same, two or three blades create more flash than a single.

Vary the color of the bait (essentially, the color of the vinyl or rubber hula skirt) according to the water clarity by using whites, light blues, and yellows in off-color water; greens, dark blues, purples, browns, and chartreuse in average water; whites again, black-and-whites, and blacks in very clear water.

Remember, too, that clear water conditions usually require the smaller lures (no matter what type) and the lighter lines. Sometimes, this calls for an open-face spinning outfit and 6- to 10-pound test lines.

Leadhead Jigs

The leadhead jig can be used in shallow to the deepest water, simply by scaling down the line and lure at the lesser depths and increasing the size of line and lure at the greatest depths.

However, it is in *deep* fishing, from 15 to 50 feet, that the leadhead jig stands out among lures. Few artificials yet designed are as effective for dredging bass out of their deep water sanctuaries. Because of its weight, the jig will sink quickly and will stay down once it does hit bottom.

The leadhead jig consists of a molded leadhead into which the shank of an upright-riding single hook is molded. Attached to the neck of the lure is a vinyl or rubber skirt. The leadhead is roughly the same shape as a spinnerbait, except for its lack of wire struts and spinner blades. The larger jigs are often made more effective by the addition of a trailer on the hook—a plastic worm, splittail worm, plastic lizard, or a piece of porkrind.

Most jig fishing is done "downhill." The lure is cast into shallower water and then worked down an incline such as a sloping point, the side of an underwater island, or the face of a cliff or bluff. When a jig is retrieved

Here the hook point on a leadhead jig is touched up with a sharpening stone to keep the point needle sharp. This sharpness helps ensure quick penetration in a fish's mouth.

uphill, the number of hangups and snags increase because the path of the lure is always *into* and *against* the slope.

One manner of fishing jigs is similar to that used in retrieving a plastic worm. The jig is cast out, allowed to settle to the bottom (again, watch for strikes as the lure is sinking), and then retrieved with a series of rod tip twitches. Generally, however, a jig is fished a little faster than a plastic worm; that is, the lifts of the rod tip are a little longer than those used in worm fishing so that the jig "hops" a foot or so each time, in contrast to the plastic worm, which moves inches at a time.

To make the jig appear more lifelike (some fishermen believe a jig hopping along the bottom resembles a crawfish), vary the number of hops by lifting the rod tip. As an example, here's one rhythm: hop/hop-hop-hop/ hop-hop. Here, the jig is pulled or hopped once, then allowed to settle back to the bottom, then is hopped three times in quick succession, then allowed to settle, then hopped twice and so on. An irregular or erratic movement is more likely to attract a bass than a regular movement of the lure. Creatures in the bass' domain usually don't travel in smooth, continuous motions; they spurt, scamper, and scramble.

The little hopping motion begins while the rod is at a 9:30 or 10 o'clock position and can be continued until almost 12 o'clock is reached. Most strikes will occur as the lure is sinking between hops. When a strike is felt, set the hook as soon as possible by dropping the rod to a strike angle (9 or 10 o'clock), quickly reeling any slack out of the line and heaving back with the rod. The whole process—drop rod, take up slack, strike—shouldn't take longer than a second. If there's one thing a bass will spit out faster than a fraudulent worm, it's a leadhead jig.

A simpler method of leadhead jig fishing, most effective in deep water, is the *start-and-stop* retrieve. This is a good method from late spring through early fall when bass will hit a faster moving offering, in contrast to the slower, hopping technique, which works well in winter.

Cast to shallower water, let the jig settle to the bottom (when a jig hits bottom, a slight bump may be felt and the line will go slack), and then start it spurting forward into deeper water by rapidly turning the reel handle a few times. Then abruptly *stop* the retrieve and let the jig settle back down. Repeat this process, varying the retrieve between two, three, and four quick handle turns each spurt, until the lure is back to the boat. Holding the rod at about a 10 o'clock angle during the retrieve will put it in a good position to set the hook immediately when a fish strikes.

Leadhead jigs can also be good vertical jigging lures, although lately many vertical jiggers have been turning to chrome spoons for this type of angling. At any rate, the jig can be fished straight down, among rocks and brush, and yo-yoed up and down a few inches off the bottom, by the angler alternately raising and lowering the rod tip. When vertical jigging, always allow the jig to sink on a *slack* line or else its falling attraction will be affected. And always be prepared for a strike on the sink.

Casting and Jigging Spoons

In the past year, a small group of Western bass anglers has turned to spoon-feeding bass, especially in the wintertime. The spoons, in this case, are most commonly ⅜- to ¾-ounce metal lures manufactured by Hopkins, Kastmaster, Dardevle, Sidewinder, and other manufacturers.

Spoons will wiggle or dart on a lift and flutter on a drop, making them a two-sided attractor to bass. Supposedly, these lures imitate a crippled shad, fluttering in its handicapped state and inviting a bass to dinner.

Fanciers of these metal lures know that the best spoon fishing often occurs in the midst of schools of shad, so locating these natural baitfish is a key to success. While shad schools can be spotted on the surface, it takes an electronic depthfinder to pick up the characteristic "blips" of the bait-fish under the surface.

Shad respond to wind action and tend to gather on the windward side of the lake when a stiff breeze comes up. If the wind direction is from east *to* west, the western shoreline will probably hold most of the shad. Good spoon fishermen know this, and they fish accordingly, working their lures with the schools.

Most commonly, spoons are either cast and retrieved or jigged vertically off the bottom. Each technique is rather basic compared to some other forms of bass angling.

The cast-and-retrieve method involves allowing the lure to sink to the bottom, then moving the rod tip upward in a short sweep from the 9 o'clock position up to about 10:30 or 11 o'clock. *If the rod tip is allowed to move past 11 o'clock, it's difficult to set the hook when a strike occurs.* (No leverage or strike angle remains when the rod is almost straight up.) After the sweep is made, the spoon is allowed to flutter back down to the bottom as the angler watches his line for any signal of a strike.

In contrast to plastic worm or leadhead jig fishing, the upward lift of the rod is usually *longer* when fishing with spoons. It is, in effect, a retrieve of: pull/sink–pull/sink–pull/sink. After the lure sinks each time on a *slack* line, the angler winds in the slack and lifts again. For some reason, strikes on a sinking spoon tend to be harder and more aggressive than those on a plastic worm or jig.

Vertical jigging requires yo-yoing the spoon a few inches off the bottom, while the line is essentially straight down from the rod tip. If the line enters the water at more than a slight angle, both the upward lift and the downward flutter of the jig will be adversely affected. My experience has been that the lure must be lifted straight up and dropped straight down to be most appealing to a bass.

Spoons are good lures to use in deep water, but their treble hooks make them susceptible to snags. To combat this, some spoon fishermen will snip off one of the trebles, leaving the other two hook points to do the job of hooking the fish. The result is a spoon which still has respectable fish-hooking qualities, but is much less likely to hang up in brush or rocks. Since spoons have concentrated weight, they can often be freed when they do snag by jiggling them loose with the rod and moving their weight around as a counterbalance. Be sure to allow a bit of slack line, though, to create the jiggling effect.

Crankplugs

Crankplug (so called because it is basically a cast-and-crank lure) is a term adopted by modern Western bass anglers to describe the new designs of older lures once commonly called *bass plugs* or *casting plugs*.

The popularity of the bass plug, once the traditional lure of the bass angler, decreased significantly with the introduction of the plastic worm. Anglers were suddenly turning to the worm—a relatively inexpensive and

A lot of research, design and field testing goes into
new crankplugs like these "Teeny-Rs" by Rebel before
you see them on the market.

highly effective form of lure—in place of the plugs, which cost much more
and did not have the appeal of being a new "hot" lure.

But plugs were never forgotten. In the late 1960s and early 1970s,
when big-money tournament bass anglers began to plan their fishing
strategies, they turned to the old standby plug, or crankplug, because this
lure is highly effective in shallow to 15-foot depths and because it also
covers a lot of water in a short amount of time. When some major tournaments were won by anglers tossing crankplugs, other bass fishermen
began to notice and the trend started to reverse.

One of the earliest of these tourney superstars was the Big-O plug, a
lure described by some observers as a pregnant guppy because of its fat,
rounded body. Since tournament fishing was now dictating what the
average bass angler would buy . . . and try . . . a rush on Big-Os followed,
and demand far exceeded supply for some time. Other tackle manufacturers, predicting the rebirth of plug casting, soon produced similar lures,
leading to the era of the "alphabet" plugs. These were called alphabet
plugs because among the choices offered by manufacturers were the
Big-O, the Balsa-B, the Big-N, and the Little-R. Since the rebirth of

crankplugs, many other variations of the first alphabet-type lures have been successfully introduced, and the list is still growing.

Most of these crankplugs have basic similarities. Most are pulled down to their designed running depths by the action of water passing over a diving bill (an angled plane surface) molded or attached to the lower, front portion of the plug body. Most crankplugs are made of a molded plastic shell which makes them buoyant when at rest. (The Bagley Bait Company's crankplugs, however, are made of balsa wood and are extremely fine lures.) Many of the crankplugs now being manufactured also have a relatively fat forward section and concave sides and taper off to a thinner tail section. Armament is usually via one belly treble hook and one tail treble hook.

What's responsible for the popularity of crankplugs today, besides that initial tournament publicity? Three factors may account for the lures' popularity and effectiveness.

First, when the Big-O lures became popular, they offered a *different* action from that of many of the previous casting plugs. The side-to-side swimming range of the newer versions was, in many cases, shortened, producing a more frantic wiggle in a quicker stroke. It's like comparing a saunter to a nervous twitch. The alphabet plugs appeared much more agitated to me and probably to bass, too. (1)

Second, redesigned diving bills on these lures took the plugs deeper— from the surface to their deepest depth—in a very short period of time. Fewer turns of the reel handle were required to get the lures down, resulting in more bass territory covered per retrieve. In the old days of plug casting, only a few lures such as the Heddon Go-Deeper, the Bomber, the Bomber Waterdog, and the Hellbender really went down to that prime bass country. Today, there are many crankplugs which will zip down to 12 or 15 feet. Some, used with high-retrieve reels, will even reach 20 feet or more. (2)

Third, a resurgence in plug fishing could be tied to anglers discovering that plugs were important in the bass fisherman's strategy. Few lures can be cast and retrieved more quickly to cover more water than a crankplug; they are excellent lures to use when the fisherman is faced with unfamiliar shoreline territory and is looking for concentrated numbers of fish. Consider that it could take more than an hour to work a 50-yard stretch of shore carefully, while flipping a plastic worm. In contrast, the crankplugger, working on the theory that he'll eventually locate fish if he covers enough water, could cover 50 yards in 15 to 20 minutes. (3)

This ability to cover ground quickly is one of the single greatest advantages to the crankplug angler. His beliefs are:

1.   There are *always some* bass present in shallow water.
2.   Shallow water bass are usually *feeding*, or striking, bass.
3.   If *enough* shoreline area is fished and *enough* casts are made, a

crankplug fisherman will locate bass by the end of the day.

This practice of methodically working shoreline cover and maximizing the number of lure presentations (casts) in a day has given the crankplug the name *percentage bait*, for its supporters believe that blanketing the water with casts will always produce a certain percentage of the fish.

As with other types of lures, crankplugs used in the shallowest water, down to 6 feet, are often most effective in the smaller sizes and weights and on the lighter lines.

The crankplug is an excellent "edge" lure—that is, it is cast near a target so it will dive and run along the edge of the target, where a bass could be holding. Strikes often occur as the lure is running alongside a piece of brush, tree trunk, rocks, or old fence row. When casting to these targets, always make sure you cast far enough *behind* the target so that the lure will dive to its designed depth and wiggle as it passes the target.

Because of their ability to dive quickly, crankplugs are also good bets to retrieve down or parallel to a fast-sloping shore, such as the shallow-water portion of a land point dipping into a lake. By casting the plug into the shallower water and then increasing the retrieve speed as the lure works down, you can keep the plug hugging the bottom for quite a distance, at least until its maximum depth is achieved. Crankplugs can also be effective when cast to cliffs and bluffs, but the plug must be cast *within inches* of the cliff or bluff face because bass will hold very close to the face.

It's difficult to say just how many casts a crankplug fisherman should make to one spot before moving on to the next, but here are a few suggestions for *minimum* numbers of casts:

Points of land—Make at least 6 casts at good-looking points—one down the top of the point, one shallow on the left side, one deeper on the left side, one each shallow and deeper on the right side, and one *across* the exposed tip of the point.

A single piece of brush—One cast on each side of the stickup so that the plug passes within a foot of the brush.

Brushy area—One well-placed cast into each likely-looking open pocket in the brush; two casts in especially good-looking spots.

Old fence row—One cast along each side of row, retrieved parallel to the fence posts.

Large, exposed rock—At least three casts; one cast parallel along each side and one cast to the point of the rock extending farthest into the lake.

These examples aren't intended to suggest that crankplug fishing can be rigidly confined to an exact number of casts per particular spot, but that too many casts at one spot can waste fishing time. The crankplug is a "locator" lure, and you have to keep moving at a reasonable pace to find fish. When you're fishing your own favorite areas of a lake, you may want to invest more fishing time and casts in these locations.

Always use the fastest retrieve speed possible with the larger crankplugs to make the lure dive quickly to its maximum depth. Then, you may find, depending on the model of your crankplug, that you can decrease your retrieve speed and the plug will maintain its deepest running range. Because of sizes popularly varying from ⅜ to ⅝ ounce and different diving bill designs, crankplugs can be classified into shallow-running (0 to 4 feet), medium-running (4 to 10 feet), and deep-running (10 to about 18 feet, in most cases) types. Be sure to match the type you are using to the depth being fished, remembering that bass tend to be located near the bottom in shallow water. It makes little sense to be chucking a shallow-running crankplug into 15 feet of water unless you are after surface bass chasing shad. Otherwise, you're probably not going to get down to the majority of the fish.

When I'm using crankplugs, I like to hold the rod tip low, almost touching the water. I feel this gives the lure better action, helps it to stay deep, and provides a low rod angle from which to set the hook. I don't point the rod right down the line, but hold it off to my left side at about a 45-degree angle.

While crankplugs hook a lot of bass, they are also responsible for losing some fish, due to their free-swinging treble hooks. A much smaller percentage of bass seems to be lost on plastic worms, spinnerbaits, and lead-head jigs, all of which utilize *single* hooks *solidly* attached to the lures. A bass hooked on a crankplug can shake his head and flip that lure around—one of its favorite escape tactics when taking to the air—because the lure body acts as a swinging lever to loosen the hooks.

There're perhaps only two things you can do to keep your fish losses to a minimum: (1) set the hook solidly, even when you think a bass has firmly hooked itself; and (2) keep all slack out of the line and a steady pull against the fish. The least bit of slack will invite the fish to jump—and pitch the plug back at you.

Topwater Lures

Topwater lures or surface plugs can be effective when bass are in shallow water. Ranging from ¼ to ⅝ ounce, these artificials float at rest, and then splash, gurgle, pop, bob, crawl, or quiver when retrieved with short twitches of the rod tip. They are designed to look like a crippled and/or struggling creature on the surface of the water—an injured minnow or shad, a frog, small bass or panfish, and a few forms which don't resemble anything in the lake.

Some anglers consider topwater artificials to be limited lures and, as these do require patience to fish properly, they sometimes prefer other shallow water lures. Little over a decade ago, topwaters were still one of the standby baits of a lot of anglers, but their popularity has waned, at least on some lakes. Shallow reservoirs with areas of abundant aquatic growth probably still yield a lot of largemouths which are hooked by surface plugs casters. But the trend toward plastic worms, spinnerbaits, crank-plugs, and even lightweight jigs—all effective in shallow areas—has probably contributed to the decreased use of surface plugs.

I'm not saying that topwater lures are not in use today or that they won't catch fish, because both cases are certainly true. One advantage to the floating surface lure is that it basically stays *on top* of the water, making it possible to fish the lure in some otherwise impossible cover.

Let's say you want to fish an area of many submerged trees, possibly a flooded orchard, but you see no practical way to retrieve a lure *through* a maze of overlapping branches. With a surface plug, you don't have to go through, you can go *over* the snags. Of course, if a bass takes the lure you'll have to hope you can hold it or bust it out of the obstacles before it tangles the line. Because of their value in the snag-infested shallows, surface plugs also work well around lily-pad beds, heavy brush, tules, and similar habitat.

If the plastic worm angler is the master of finesse under the water, the serious topwater-lure tosser is the artisan above the water. To fish surface lures properly, you have to be patient and delicate, and it's on those two points which many fishermen fail.

Few surface plugs are very effective if cast and then retrieved *immediately* after splashdown. It's best to let the lure lay still briefly so it looks as if the creature has landed on the water and is stunned. This waiting period can vary from only 15 seconds up to most of a minute. Its length depends on the size of the lure (I wait a longer time with larger plugs), the noise of the splash (if it makes a commotion, I wait longer to give a spooked fish a chance to settle down), the calmness of the water (wait longer in glassy water) and the biting mood of the fish (very actively feeding fish seem to hit sooner).

A rule of thumb once offered was wait until all of the ripples disappear from the water, following the splashdown; however, I've taken a lot of topwater bass, cutting that time down slightly.

Some topwater lures have propellers which turn on retrieve; some pencil-popper types have no propellers; other surface plugs have large concave surfaces on their heads which scoop the water; and still others utilize a forward-mounted wiggle-plate which makes the lure crawl on retrieve.

In most cases, the key to properly retrieving a topwater model is to produce a *delicate, erratic* motion of the lure, using the rod tip to create a struggling effect. You want to make it barely wiggle or flutter or dance. This should be accomplished with a fairly tight line, too, as excess slack will make it much more difficult to set the hook when a fish strikes.

Vary the number of rod twitches, from one to three or four in quick succession, then pause a few seconds before twitching the lure again. In

*Using the rod tip to work the lure, John Alexander
of Lake Havasu City, Arizona, practices vertical
jigging in deep water.*

addition to varying the number of twitches each time, vary the length of time between the series of twitches. The idea is to create an erratic movement, not a predictable rhythm. You want to make a bass think it's getting a free meal.

Casting accuracy is very important, too. You should practice until you can drop your lure right on target, at least 8 out of 10 times. When working a brush-choked area, for instance, you may be aiming for small openings only a few feet in diameter and, of course, if you have to move the boat over to a spot where a lure is snagged, you'll probably spook any bass in that area.

That brings up another advantage of having more than one fishing outfit. On several occasions I've been surface fishing a spot, caught several fish, and, unfortunately, flipped a cast into a snag. Instead of immediately rushing over to free the lure, I've let it remain there until I've worked all the *surrounding* area with a second rod-and-reel outfit. This way I've often taken a few more bass, that certainly would have fled if I had tried to retrieve the first lure before I was finished fishing there.

I should mention a point about safety. Because surface plugs are often

These propeller-type topwater plugs create a surface disturbance when twitched by the rod tip. When the prop turns it creates the noise and appearance of an injured baitfish.

outfitted with two or three good-size treble hooks and because the lures are used *above* the water, they can easily come flying back your way if you pull forcefully to free a snagged lure. I free the lure by gently flipping the rod tip so if the plug does come free, it won't come flying all the way back to the boat . . . and directly at me. If it won't come loose by gentle flipping, I play it safe and move the boat over to the lure. A couple of large treble hooks sticking in the human body can do some nasty damage.

Surface fishing is exciting because so much of the fight is visual—either right on the surface, in midair as the fish jumps, or just under the surface. It's a real adrenalin-pumper to see a 5-pound bass walloping a topwater offering, then taking to the air and turning acrobat in its attempts to throw the plug. Setting the hook as soon as possible and keeping the line tight at all times are especially important with these lures because, as with crankplugs, the fish has the advantage and leverage of free-swinging hooks.

This bass mistook a live waterdog for an easy meal.
Waterdogs are particularly effective on some of the
large lakes of the West.

4

Fishing With Wigglies

Live bait can produce some lively bass fishing.

I've found times when bass, or at least most of them, refused a battery of lures designed to trigger their feeding instinct and coax them into striking. But when presented with a live wiggly, those same fish ended up committing suicide on a hook.

This has happened often enough so that I do occasionally use live bait, even though I prefer catching fish on artificial lures. When the fish become finicky and pass up the frauds, I believe in being flexible and giving them what they want.

Just a few weeks ago my family made a trip to a large Western lake which, according to some fishermen who had recently fished there, was producing "poor" bass catches. In fact, a major bass fishing tournament was held there a week before we arrived, and 170 skilled bass anglers caught less than a dozen limits of bass (7 fish) a day for the three days of the event. So fishing did indeed appear "slow."

Of course, tournament contestants were not permitted to use live bait, so all of the tourney fish were taken on artificial lures. We then visited an area of the lake that had been heavily fished during the tournament, and four of us caught 98 bass in three days! And we fished only a few hours a day.

What was the difference? Well, no one knows for certain, but I suspect we had such grand luck mainly because we were using live waterdogs, those wiggly, slippery salamanders that bass seem to find irresistible. Someone suggested that we had merely arrived at the lake just as the bass began "turning on" and lure fishermen at the same time could have made similar fine catches. I can't dispute that possibility. I can only say that we've made seven, multiday, fall trips to this lake, each time using live waterdogs as the principal bait, and we haven't failed yet to find excellent fishing—no matter what the rating of the lake was at the time.

Further evidence of the effectiveness of live bait can be inferred from the catches of Florida-strain bass in the San Diego City lakes system. The big Floridas show a definite preference for live baits—principally craw-dads, nightcrawlers, waterdogs, or mudsuckers—and many of the pro San Diego bass chasers have become masters of the live wigglies. The California state-record bass, which is also the second-largest largemouth ever caught *in the world*, was hooked on a live nightcrawler in a San Diego lake. That fish weighed 20 pounds and 15 ounces.

There are, however, some disadvantages to live bait fishing, and I should point them out here.

Three Disadvantages of bait fishing ↓

First, bass hooked on live bait will sometimes take the bait deep into their gullet or stomach, and this makes it difficult, in good conscience, to release small fish. A lip-hooked bass, taken on artificials, is more likely to survive than one hooked deep via live bait.

Second, live bait is more non-discriminating than a bass lure. You may occasionally catch another type of fish on a bass-designed artificial, but you'll more often catch those other types on live bait, as bluegill, crappie, catfish, trout, and others will strike the wigglies.

Third, fishing with live bait requires a little more tackle rigging time and, of course, you usually have to pin a new bait on your hook each time after catching a fish. When lure fishing, you don't need to re-bait.

That's the bad news.

Advantages

The good news is that there are those times when live bait is the most effective morsel you can put on the end of your line. And catching bass on live bait, to me, is more fun than catching nothing or very little on artificials.

Waterdogs

As I've mentioned, the live waterdog can be a devastating bait for bass. I've had my best luck with waterdogs in the 4- to 5-inch range, as 'dogs shorter than this seem to attract many other smaller fish.

A good way to fish the live waterdog is to keep your rigging gear to a *minimum*. The less hardware hanging on the line, the less the chances of spooking a bass. All that is usually needed is a 1/0 or 2/0 long shank hook tied to the end of the monofilament line and just enough splitshot pinched on the line about 30 inches up from the hook to take the bait to the bottom.

The splitshot weight may vary according to the fishing conditions. If you are drift fishing and a stiff breeze is blowing, you'll have to increase the weight of the splitshot for the bait to reach the bottom and *stay down* as the boat is drifting; the faster the drift, the more weight necessary. You may even have to use a sliding, egg-shape sinker on the line, held in place by a splitshot 30 inches up from the hook. Still, in most instances just a small splitshot is adequate, so don't overweight the rig.

The secret to waterdog fishing is to keep the bait moving. If the waterdog is allowed to rest too long in one place, it has a habit of crawling into or under a snag. Instead of letting the bait just soak on the bottom, move it slightly toward the boat every few seconds, much the same way you would retrieve a plastic worm. This not only makes the bait more visible to bass which may be some distance away, it also significantly decreases the number of snags and lost hooks and sinkers.

At times, when bass are shallow and a suspended school is found, it's possible to use no sinker at all. The waterdog is simply pinned on the hook and "fly lined" out to the fish, the bass often hitting the 'dog as it is sinking.

I once read an article on waterdog fishing in which the author recommended hooking the waterdog through its lips, inserting the hook point in the *upper* lip of the bait and passing it out the *lower* lip. Maybe that method works for other people, but it has never worked for me or anyone else I've ever seen use these salamanders. With the hook imbedded in that direction, the point would be down, the same as if the hook on a spinnerbait or leadhead jig were reversed, and would always be *digging into the bottom of the lake*. No wonder he said in this article that waterdogs often snag.

A much better method is to hook the dog through both lips, inserting the hook point in the *bottom* lip first and then through the top, so the hook point rides *up*.

As bass usually hit these baits aggressively, it's fine to fish with the reel in gear, instead of giving the fish line to swim off and swallow the bait. Wait until the strikes of the fish become sharp and the bass begins to take the rod tip down. When you feel the line get tight or "heavy" and the rod tip starts to dip, raise the rod sharply and set the hook. If necessary, take up a little line to get a good rod strike angle before you drive in the hook.

Also, fishing with the reel in gear will drastically decrease the number of deep-hooked fish. The majority of the bass will have the hook in their lips, which conserves small fish you may want to release.

Veteran waterdog fishermen don't merely drop their bait straight down and wait for a fish to happen along, either. They actively *cast and slow-retrieve* waterdogs to and from selected targets, just as if they were tossing a lure. They work as hard at waterdogging as crankplug fishermen work at their craft, and it's every bit as much an art to be a good waterdog man.

Nightcrawlers

The live nightcrawler will catch almost anything. It is a smaller bait and, because of its soft shape, will bunch up and fit into the mouths of crappie, bluegill, perch, spotted bass, striped bass, pike, carp, trout—you

name it and a nightcrawler will take it. It's not a highly selective bait, but it
is quite effective for bass.

Again, keep the rigging as simple as possible to minimize the chance of
spooking a bass. Nightcrawlers can be used with a size 1 through 4 hook,
and the weight should consist only of a splitshot attached to the line about
30 inches up from the hook.

My favorite rigging method is to hook the 'crawler once or twice on the
hook, passing the hook point through the bait in its *midsection*. This leaves
both ends free to wiggle enticingly and attract a bass. I've also found that
liberal use of this bait—using two nightcrawlers on a hook instead of just
one—seems to catch more bass. Possibly, this is because the pair of nightcrawlers appears to be a big gob of food, with *four* wiggling ends.

If you purchase live nightcrawlers for bait, always check at the time
you buy them to make certain they are in good condition. Most bait-and-
tackle shop people dump out the contents of the 'crawler carton and show
you the bait is prime, but if they don't and you don't check, you'll be
taking a chance when you later pop the lid. It's disappointing to find that
your live bait has been dead for a week.

*Live mudsuckers can be used for bass. The bait should
be pinned through the lips, with the hook point inserted
in the bottom lip and out the top lip.*

One way to hook a crawdad is to push the hook point into the bottom of the third tail-segment, then out the top.

Nightcrawlers can be fished in three ways: (1) still-fished, with the bait remaining in one place; (2) worked slowly along the bottom, with the rod tip held high to minimize snags; or (3) drift-fished. Moving the bait slowly along the bottom probably increases its chances of passing close to a bass, but because so much of the hook is exposed, it also increases the chances of the hook hanging on the bottom. I've taken bass using each of the three methods and have no real favorite; it all depends on what the bass prefer at any given time.

Nightcrawlers can also be fished "in gear," although some anglers like to give a striking bass some freespooled line to allow the fish to swallow the bait. Usually, a bass sucks in a 'crawler in one vacuum motion, so additional line isn't necessary. Either method will work, but striking at the first "heavy" pull, with the reel in gear, will produce more lip-hooked fish and conserve more small, throw-back-size bass.

By the way, small bass can still be released even if they have deeply swallowed the hook. Without even lifting the fish into the boat, reach over the side and cut your line at the point where it just comes out of the fish's mouth. There's a good chance the fish will not be badly injured and, due to the gastric acids produced by the fish, the hook will rust out in a fairly short time.

Crawdads

Crawdads are deadly for bass, especially big bass.

Personally, I like 'dads about 3 inches long for bass fishing; that's long enough to interest a decent-size fish, yet not so large that the fish has difficulty taking the bait and you have difficulty deciding when to set the hook.

The rigging is as simple as that for waterdogs or nightcrawlers—a hook tied on the end of the line, followed by just enough splitshot to take the rig to the bottom. The long shank hooks range from size 1 to 2/0, depending on the size of the bait.

The crawdad can either be hooked through the head, with the hook point entering below the head and coming out through the bridge of exo-skeleton just forward of the creature's eyes, or it can be hooked through the tail, inserting the hook into the *bottom* of the third segment of the tail and pushing the point out through the top.

The crawdad can be highly effective when cast out and slowly twitched along the bottom, as if it were a plastic worm. Or, if you're fishing a definite bass hole, it may be still-fished. Some fishermen like to twist off the pinchers of the bait to make it more snag-resistant, but I prefer to use the crawdad in its most natural form, with pinchers attached. This is just a matter of personal preference.

However, with this type of bait I do not keep the reel in gear once I feel a strike. As this bait has a tougher outer covering (an exo-skeleton) than other bass baits, the bass has to mash that 'dad around a few seconds in its mouth, and I let the fish do that without feeling the resistance of a tight line. When I feel a strike, I immediately put the reel in freespool and let the bass swim off 5 or 6 feet with the bait. Then I switch the reel back into gear, wait for the bass to take any slack out of the line, and try to tear the fish's head off.

Other Baits

LIVE MUDSUCKERS will also catch bass. They can be rigged identically to the other live baits—with a hook and a just-sufficient amount of splitshot—or they can be "fly lined" without a sinker on the line. Because they live in saltwater, however, the bait must be kept in the water provided with them at the time of purchase. After a live mudsucker has been on a hook in freshwater for a time, its gills swell and it will eventually die. It's not as hardy or as easily cared for as most other natural baits, and its slippery skin and tough head makes it more difficult to pin on a hook. When hooking the bait, pin it through its lips, from lower lip up through the top one, just like a waterdog.

MINNOWS will also take bass, but must be kept in cool, aerated water during hot weather or they will weaken or die. My use of live minnows has been limited because I've usually preferred other types of natural bait. When I have used minnows, I've used them without any weight, allowing the bait to swim naturally in the water. The reel should be in freespool, so a bass striking the minnow can swim off for a few feet before you set the hook. The minnow can be hooked either through its lips or by inserting the hook just below the base of the dorsal fin.

RED WORMS are not recommended as live bait for serious bass fishermen. These worms are so small they will catch almost anything, and you may be constantly catching bluegill, crappie, small catfish, or bass so small that most should be thrown back in the water.

Live bait can produce big bass, like this
9-pounder taken on a nightcrawler at Lake Mohave
on the Colorado River.

Bass will often lie next to a structure in shallow water such
as these partially submerged trees. In this case, lures should be
cast several feet behind the tree, then retrieved alongside the trunk.

5

Western Bass Structures

Bass are where you find them, and finding them isn't always easy.

Many good bass fishermen believe (and I agree) that *locating* bass is usually more difficult than *catching* them. There are many theories on where to find bass, some of which propose fishing deeper in winter, fishing shady areas on bright, sunny days, and fishing shallow early and late in the day. Many times these rules work—and sometimes they don't.

Recent research on largemouth bass behavior suggests that bass may be much more independent than we previously thought; they appear to display highly individual behavior. Through the use of sonar transmitters implanted in bass, fishery biologists are tracking the movements of fish and finding that while some bass do move a great deal, others move very little; while some bass prefer shallow water, others stay in deep water most of the year; while some bass prefer rocky structures, others are attracted to brushy areas; and though some bass are shoreline fish, others will suspend in water in the middle of the lake.

The early results of such research seem to indicate that we, as fishermen, don't know as much as we thought or else that bass fishing is becoming more confusing than ever. Or both.

And that's why bass are where you find them.

But though there are no hard-and-fast rules for locating bass, there are certain factors which influence where they may be found.

First, let's consider the basic requirements of bass. They need three things: (1) an area of proper water temperature; (2) some type of cover from which the bass can dart out and ambush its prey; and (3) an area close to deep water, so the bass can escape to safety if it feels threatened.

Biologists tell us that bass prefer 66- to 75-degree water temperature, the ideal temperature being around 70 degrees. At these temperatures, the metabolism of the bass is in high gear and the fish is most actively moving and feeding. And since not all areas or levels of a lake will be the same temperature at the same time, one step toward locating bass is to own and use a good water thermometer. By checking the water in several areas, you can locate the depth at which the most suitable temperatures are present and fish accordingly.

Finding the areas of preferred water temperatures is only one step in locating bass. What happens if 70-degree water is present in several areas of a lake and in a broad range of depths? Surely that leaves a lot of territory to search and most of it will probably be fishless. To narrow down the hunt, we look for bass structure.

Structure is another term which grew out of bass fishing tournaments. Tournament pros began referring to bass structure, underwater structure, natural structure, manmade structure, and visible structure. Of course, other bass anglers had been talking about structure for many years prior, but then they called it "cover" or "habitat."

Broadly defined, structure can be any feature of a lake, from a single brushpile to a long, submerged river channel, which attracts bass. You could almost say that structure is anything which makes a lake something other than a flat-bottomed reservoir; structure gives a change in contour to an otherwise plain, homogenous area. An underwater island would be structure, because it *rises up* from the lake bottom and creates a *change* in the surrounding terrain. A tree standing in the water would be structure for the same reason. Similarly, rockslides, points of land jutting into the lake, docks, reefs, deep holes, and lily-pad beds are all bass structures.

Bass are attracted to structure for the three reasons listed at the beginning of this chapter: temperature, food, and escape to deep water. Structures can be divided into three general types:

1.   Natural, visible structure, which is at least partly above water and usually near shore.

2.   Natural, invisible structure, which is below the water and may be relatively far from shore.

3.   Manmade structure.

Natural, Visible Structures

The following are some of the most productive visible structures:

FLOATING LILY PADS are good structure areas. Fish the open pockets of the pads, the points of the beds, and the edges closest to deep water. Due to the shade afforded by the dense plants, lily-pad beds are especially good areas to fish in the heat of summer. Topwater lures, weedless spoons, and Texas-rigged plastic worms are usually the most snag-resistant artificials to use around the heavy growth.

POINTS OF LAND sloping off into the lake attract bass. A point often produces well when it is fished uphill (from deep to shallow water) with a plastic worm or downhill with a leadhead jig. Crankplugs are also good bets to cast parallel to the sides of the point or across its tip. Especially good points are those of broken rock with 35- to 50-degree angles of slope into the lake.

Some points have a deep-water side and a shallow-water side; usually the deep-water side produces more fish. Points tend to be good holding areas for bass throughout the day, as the fish will move up the point into the shallows in the morning and late afternoon, and down the point into deeper water during the day.

CLIFFS OR BLUFFS are usually adjacent to deep water and often produce bass holding very tight to the structure. If the water is very deep, the bass could be suspended; that is, they may be only 25 feet deep along the bluffs, even though the depth there is 60 feet. Use leadhead jigs, live bait, and plastic worms and be especially alert for strikes as the offering is sinking.

Irregularities in cliffs or bluff faces could be called substructures located within a structure. The irregularities—cracks, crevices, and pockets —attract bass. Cliffs or bluffs are good summer and winter structures.

SHALLOW WATER STICKUPS consist of brush, weeds, small trees, tules, or other vegetation which provides cover for bass and offers them an ambush site. Stickups always hold *some* fish in the shallows, but the number will vary greatly.

Stickups can be fished with a wide variety of bass lures and live bait, and springtime spinnerbait fishing often is the best method for catching bass. Topwater lures, of course, are a prime choice for fishing shallow-water stickups.

FALLEN TREES in the lake create potential homes for bass. The fish may be lying under the tree or alongside of it, and they usually won't move far from their protective covering to hit a lure. To avoid spooking wary fish, first work the deepest part of the tree, the portion farthest from shore. Then edge in cautiously to fish the shallow-water portion. Try topwater lures, live bait, weedless spoons, plastic worms, or a jig worked vertically among the branches.

Natural, Invisible Structures

Several types of invisible, underwater structure, create good bass fishing spots.

OLD RIVER OR CREEK CHANNELS provide some excellent bass fishing, especially in the summer and winter. The outside bends of the channels normally hold the most and largest bass. Channels which contain both rocks and brush are especially inviting and can produce some excellent fishing on plastic worms, live baits, leadhead jigs, and deep-trolled plugs.

SUBMERGED TREES also beckon to bass. Try spinnerbaits and cast them close to the trees, then allow them to flutter-sink alongside the trees. Underwater trees must be fished closely, since bass usually won't move far in this habitat to strike their prey. Stands of old sunken trees provide good structure for working vertical jigging spoons, especially in winter.

ROCKPILES are good bass-attracting areas, even more so if brush is present, too. Give special attention to points of submerged rockpiles, where they drop off into deeper water. Work jigs and plastic worms downhill; work plugs parallel to the structure; and, if the top of the rockpile is 10 feet deep or less, try topwater lures over the top of the mound all day in the spring, or early and late in the day during the summer.

UNDERWATER ISLANDS AND REEFS are worth fishing, too. Fish the sloping sides of the structure with plastic worms, live baits, crankplugs, spinnerbaits, leadhead jigs, or spoons. Try the top of the structure with crankplugs or, if the depth allows, surface lures. You can often locate an island or reef by tracking out a long-running point from shore.

ROCKSLIDES can often be discovered by noting areas of shoreline where slides have sloughed off rocks into the water. Rockslides are most common in deep lakes which have areas of cliffs and bluffs along shore. Deep-running crankplugs, plastic worms, jigs, and spinnerbaits rank among the best lures for this bass habitat.

Manmade Structures

In addition to natural lake structures, bass can often be caught near artificial or manmade structures.

THE FACE OF A DAM may hold bass if the dam is constructed of concrete or rock riprap. Earthen dams, with their homogenous surfaces, usually don't produce many fish. Lures which stay on the bottom usually work well here because of the acute slope of the dam. Try plastic worms, spinnerbaits, and leadhead jigs. If rocky and steep, the shoreline immediately adjacent to each side of the dam should be fished, too.

OLD DOCK PILINGS are good bets, especially if located in less-fished areas. Cast lures alongside the pilings and retrieve them parallel to the structures.

FENCE ROWS should be fished in the same manner, casting alongside and bringing the lure back parallel to the row of posts.

OLD ROADBEDS, submerged when a lake was filled, may hold bass attracted to the side slopes of an *elevated* roadbed—a flat roadbed isn't considered prime bass structure. Use spinnerbaits, plugs, spoons, or live bait in shallow areas; leadhead jigs, plastic worms, or live bait in deep water areas.

Shoreline vegetation makes good bass habitat.
These anglers are working the fringe area of a tule
bed hoping for action.

WATER CONTROL TOWERS, located near the dam in many lakes, will sometimes hold bass, although usually singles and not school fish. Use a lure likely to be hit while it sinks, such as a leadhead jig or spinnerbait, or "fly line" a live bait without a sinker alongside the tower.

WATER INLET STRUCTURES, such as large concrete pipes, chutes or spillways, are found in some reservoirs. Bass may be found near the structures in a bottom depression (deep hole) made by the continual flow of water washing out the lake bottom.

(By the way, at this writing the Umco Corporation, which manufactures a quality line of tackle boxes, offers fishermen a free, four-color poster of bass fishing structures. To obtain one, drop a line to: Umco Corporation, Box 608, Highway 25, Watertown, Minnesota 55388.)

Bass Patterns

Many skilled fishermen believe a significant percentage of the bass will follow a "pattern" on any particular day (admitting that the pattern may change daily or even hourly) and that if they can discover that pattern, they will more quickly take good catches. "Pattern" refers to the type of cover, depth, and lure or bait the bass prefer at any given time.

If a pattern fisherman was fishing a variety of structures and lures and caught two bass on a crankplug in about 15 feet of water off a brushy point and three bass in another spot on the same type of structure and lure and in the same depth—without taking any fish on other structure or on other lures—he would deduce that the combination crankplug-15 feet-brush point was the pattern. He would then adapt his fishing to include *only* those elements; he would start looking for other areas in the lake that contained brushy points in about 15 feet of water. Supposedly, this combination would work as long as the fish remained in that pattern.

Personally, I've found that on many days there are several patterns in effect on the same lake. That is, I've compared notes with other successful fishermen and found that they took their fish at different depths, on different lures, and on different structures. Like so much in fishing, pattern fishing is theoretical and any lake is filled with exceptions. However, pattern fishing does at least provide a framework of fishing strategy.

I think if there's one rule to remember in locating bass, it is that the largemouth is basically a "next-to" fish. He is likely going to be found *next to* something—whether it's a piece of brush, a rock, a piling, or a point. If you just think in terms of looking for a hiding place, you'll bushwhack some bass.

6

Tips For Taking Western Bass

Several Western bass fishermen I know possess a wealth of experience and information which can be useful to beginning or intermediate anglers. Following are some suggestions which I have obtained in recent years by interviewing these skilled individuals.

DOUG "RIP" NUNNERY, a member of the Western Bass Fishing Association (WBFA), also holds the one-day record for a Bass Anglers Sportsman Society (BASS) tournament with 98 pounds and 13 ounces of bass. His advice was:

"If you want to catch a really big fish, there are generally three things to remember. Fish deep, use a plastic worm or leadhead jig, and work it slow. Small bass like shallow water, but a big bass spends most of his time in water from 18 to 40 feet deep. The big ones would rather lay in a deeper spot and wait for food to come to them than chase baitfish all over the lake.

"When you're after big fish, use a slower retrieve in the winter when the bass' metabolism slows down and he's less active. Use a faster retrieve in summer.

"The top three lures I've found are the 6-inch plastic worm, the jig-and-eel combination, and the spinnerbait. And I catch a lot of fish on purple, black, and blue lures."

DON SIEFERT, a member of WBFA who has landed several bass in the 8-pounds-and-larger class, said:

"Most people don't realize that a bass is not like a crappie or a trout. It doesn't randomly roam around a lake, but follows fairly predictable patterns. A bass feeds in certain areas for a reason, goes deeper in the summer and winter for a reason, spawns at a particular time for a reason, and sulks for a reason.

"You can learn a lot about bass fishing by studying books, talking to other fishermen, and buying a lot of sophisticated gear, but too many

Catches of largemouth bass like these are possible by using some of the experts' tips.

people believe this is *all* there is to it. They try to take the shortcut to bass fishing, when there really isn't any.

"Reading and studying books helps, sure, but if a guy really wants to learn the habits and patterns of bass he should start out at *one* lake and stick with it. Pick a lake where the bass fishing is known to be good, fish it steadily, and try to see what the successful anglers are doing. The lake should have a fairly stable water level and a variety of bass habitat.

"See where the guides are fishing, or even spend some money to go fishing with a guide one day. The investment can pay itself back many times in experience."

BILL HADDOCK, now deceased, helped pioneer the use of leadhead jigs in the West and had his own fishing tackle company, famous for its Haddock Lures. In his opinion:

"Fishing with leadhead jigs is one of the most artful forms of fishing there is. The jig isn't something you just pitch out and crank back to the boat, so that's where a lot of people go wrong. It takes patience and skill to work a jig properly.

"The jigs with revolving spinners work best in the wintertime when it takes more attraction to get Mr. Bass to strike. Use the regular (non-spinnered) jigs for spring through fall. Normally, any jig works best when fished 'downhill,' casting to shallow water and working the jig toward deep water.

"There're lots of different retrieves, but almost all of them make the jig hop in some way and then sink back to the bottom. A lot of strikes come when the jig is sinking, so you've got to be able to detect a slight twitch or hop in the line if you're going to catch bass on a jig.

"The main thing is to keep experimenting until you find what the fish want. Try different speeds, different weights of jig heads, different rhythms of retrieve, and different colors. Also, adding a 3½-inch to 5-inch strip of pork rind behind the jig will often improve its appeal."

JERRY DRONSKY has held memberships in both WBFA and in the Southern California Bassmasters. An excellent plastic worm and leadhead jig fisherman, he felt:

"Too many people think they can start fishing a lake whenever they want to and quit fishing whenever they want to . . . instead of when it's best to catch bass. Well, that doesn't work. To consistently catch bass, you should fish from as early as possible to as late as possible. You've got to cater to the whims of the *fish*, not the *fisherman*.

"Not being prepared when you do find fish is another common mistake. It's a time both you and your equipment must be prepared for. Frayed line, an improperly adjusted reel drag, or a poorly positioned boat can cost you a fish. I've even seen people lose a good fish because a tackle box was placed on top of the landing net.

"Probably one of the most common errors is being too noisy. You don't have to jump up and down in the boat to be too noisy. You can do so quite innocently if you're careless in closing tackle box lids, clanging fish stringers on the side of the boat, or tossing the net into the boat after landing a fish."

JOHN KUROVSKY, a veteran angler who has taken most species of game fish on the West Coast, offered:

"Most guys worry about what type of lure the fish are hitting, and not about *how the lure is fished*. That's not right. Some of the most deadly fish-catchers to gain popularity in recent years, like the plastic worm and the leadhead jig, don't have *any* built-in action. You've got to learn to feel what this type of lure is doing on the bottom; a good bass fisherman can work a jig or plastic worm along the bottom and tell if the lure is passing through rocks, weeds, stickups, or whatever, just by the feel coming up the line.

"You can get *the idea* of a proper worm or jig retrieve by watching other fishermen, but the only way to really become proficient with these is to fish yourself.

"After fishing steadily for some time, you'll begin to develop what the pros call a fine touch, an ability to detect an almost imperceptible twitch on the line when you're using a worm or a jig. One good way to improve your feel is to hold the fishing line between your thumb and forefinger while you twitch the rod tip.

"And every serious bass angler should have at least three outfits—one rigged for topwater or shallow fishing, one rigged for medium-depth fishing, and one rigged for deep-water fishing—or he'll spend more time changing lures and less time fishing for bass."

BERNIE SHERMAN, a veteran bass angler and a member of WBFA, contributed this:

"Being quiet is greatly underrated in bass fishing. A bass has a tendency to spook easily, and the quieter you come up on an area, the less chance you have of spooking fish.

"One thing a guy should do is put some sort of soft padding on the bottom of his tackle box, so that shuffling or sliding the box around in the boat won't send out vibrations to scare the fish. Also, the gear should be loaded in the boat so that you can get at everything easily, without having to crawl over your tackle. Accidentally knocking something off a boat seat can make enough noise to cost you a good catch.

"I have my own boat completely carpeted inside to cut down the noise, and I use an electric trolling motor to slip up to spots and hold the boat steady in a breeze. Another tip to remember is to lower an anchor gently when moving into a spot. People who think they can charge into a spot, throw their anchor over, and then catch bass often find that isn't the case.

"One thing I don't think is too important, though, is shutting off the outboard motor when fishing over deep-water structures. I don't think it makes any difference in noise if the motor is running or not when you're fishing in 30 feet or more of water."

BOB HAMMETT, a WBFA member, was nicknamed "Lucky Cast" one season when he caught 9 bass weighing over 8 pounds each. He had this to say:

"If I saw a guy walking up the dock with a big catch of bass the first thing I'd want to know is how deep he was fishing. This question would probably surprise a lot of fishermen, because people usually want to ask, 'What did you catch them on?'

"The thing is, there are lots of lures that will catch bass; the real trick is to *find* the fish. If a guy knows the depth the fish are in, he's got half the battle won. I've learned the type of terrain or structures bass prefer, so if I also know how deep they are, then I've automatically got two advantages over the next guy.

"My second question to the guy would be, 'What color lure did you use?' I don't care about the type of lure because I have confidence there's something in my tackle box that works. Just tell me the color.

"Then, I'd want to know what area the guy was fishing. Were the fish caught at the south end of the lake? The north end? Near the dam? Knowing the area can eliminate a lot of searching, and it tells you the type of cover the fish are seeking.

"The trouble with people placing so much emphasis on what *lure* the fish are hitting is that they tend to leave all the work of catching bass to the lure and not to what the fisherman does with the lure or where he fishes with it."

WAYNE CUMMINGS, also a WBFA member, has fished several regional and national bass tournaments as a representative for the Garcia Corporation, a major fishing tackle manufacturing company. His advice was:

"One of the most obvious observations to make about the Florida bass transplanted in Southern California, particularly the fish in the San Diego City lakes, is that so many of these fish are taken on live baits. It could be that this species just naturally prefers natural bait to artificials or it could be that live bait is very popular with Florida-bass fishermen. At any rate, if I wanted to catch a really big Florida, I'd have to go with live bait.

"I think the lake records would indicate that the best baits are crawfish, big nightcrawlers, and, where permitted, live shad. A good choice of outfit for these baits would be a light-action, bait-casting rod and reel and 10- or 12-pound test line.

"When fishing for Florida bass, you've got to remember that most of the time these fish lay in fairly tight to shore. They generally prefer water less than 20 feet deep. You'll often find the Floridas laying in close to the weeds and brush which parallel much of the shore.

"Using a plastic worm for Florida bass means trying black, blue, and purple colors, in that order, and fishing the plastic worm *very slowly*. Some anglers take from 5 to 8 minutes to work the worm back after a cast."

5 to 8 minutes

NORM DYE, WBFA member, once chased bass in Southern California, but now lives in Oregon. He offered the following seven guidelines for preparing yourself to become a good bass angler:

1. "You must have the desire to compete against other fishermen, yourself, and—most important—the bass.

2. "Being a bass fisherman, you have to possess the attitude of an explorer and a scientist. The searching and experimenting never stop.

3. "Never pattern your style, thoughts, and theories so that you can't change. Bass change from year to year, and so do good fishermen.

4. "You have to fish other lakes to be good. Each lake is different and so are the bass. This gives you flexibility.

5. "A bass fisherman has to feel confident that he will catch fish every time he goes out, otherwise he will get skunked once in a while. During any period of the day, any day, there will be a fish that will feed.

6. "It takes 3 to 5 years of hard, pleasureable work to become good,

and 50 percent of the time you won't land any fish. You can't accept defeat; you reprieve yourself by saying you learned something . . . at least what you did wrong.

7.   "A good bass fisherman will watch and learn from other pros. He will ask many questions and will learn to believe half the answers because no matter how good these pros are, they only *know* half the answers. There is no such thing as an expert bass fisherman."

*This largemouth was hooked in shallow water,
where any excessive noise from the fishermen might
have frightened it away.*

7

Bass Waters of the West

Variety is the keynote of bass fishing in the West. The West offers both crowded lakes, and waters which seldom see fishermen; it offers bass among pine trees and cacti; it has huge reservoirs and small ponds.

Here are some noteworthy bass fisheries found in the 11 Western states:

Arizona

Located about 60 miles east of Phoenix, *Roosevelt Lake* is a consistently good producer of largemouth bass. Roosevelt is the state's oldest impoundment and is reached via Arizona Highway 88. A large reservoir for this state, it contains 17,000 surface acres of water at capacity, but holds about 10,000 surface acres under normal conditions.

Because of its favorable bass habitat, Roosevelt produces a good number of larger fish. In 1956, a 14-pound, 2-ounce catch—the Arizona state record—was taken here.

Best fishing in Roosevelt occurs in the spring, as in most other Western reservoirs. Reefs, islands, ledges, rockpiles, and other underwater structures produce many of the larger fish, but must be located with an electronic depth finder. Favored lures at Roosevelt are plastic worms and lead-head jigs in deep water, spinnerbaits and surface plugs in shallow water.

The lake has launching ramps, as well as boat and motor rentals, a cafe, lodgings, an airstrip, and places to purchase fishing tackle supplies, groceries, and gas and oil.

Guide service for the lake is provided by the many licensed guides listed by the Arizona Game and Fish Department. A few of these are: J. Lee Erwin, Box 636, Roosevelt, AZ 85545; Gene Estes, Box 723, Roosevelt, AZ 85545; Louis E. Fuller, Box 701, Roosevelt, AZ 85545, and Floyd A. Preas, 1415 W. Rosemont, Phoenix, AZ 85027.

California

One of the best spots to catch a trophy-size bass in the Golden State is *San Vicente Reservoir* in San Diego County, Southern California. In the past few years, the lake has been producing over 100 bass weighing 9 pounds or more per season!

San Vicente is situated 4 miles north of the town of Lakeside and about 25 miles east of San Diego. Created by the damming of San Vicente Creek, this lake holds about 1,000 surface acres of water.

Some observers think the next world-record bass (over 22 pounds and 4 ounces) is swimming in San Vicente right now. At this date, the largest bass to come out of the reservoir was an 18-pound, 9-ounce monster taken in 1976. That same year, a new California state bass-limit record was also set when an angler caught five Florida-strain largemouths totaling 43 pounds and 14 ounces.

San Vicente normally operates on a four-days-a-week schedule from October through June, being closed the remainder of the time. March and April consistently produce more of the trophy-size bass than any other period.

Deep, rocky, and clear in many areas, San Vicente yields many of its largest bass to anglers using live baits: crawfish, shiners, waterdogs, nightcrawlers, and mudsuckers. Some large bass are also hooked on spinnerbaits, crankplugs, plastic worms, and leadhead jigs.

Rock and brush areas 18 feet deep or less hold many of the large bass, but in this shallow water the fish are very susceptible to noise and spook easily.

Why does San Vicente produce such large fish? Biologists believe the fish there enjoy a long annual growing season and thrive on warm water temperatures and stocked rainbow trout which they feed upon.

There is a good campground and recreational vehicle park located 5 miles southeast of the reservoir at Lake Jennings County Park. Accommodations at the lake include a 100-slip boat dock, lunch area, tackle shop, fishing pier, launch ramp, and cafe.

More information about San Vicente Lake may be obtained by writing: San Diego City Lakes, Conference Building, Balboa Park, San Diego, CA 92101.

Colorado

Colorado bass are smaller in size than those found at some other Western locales; however, some respectable size Colorado largemouths can be taken in *Bonny Reservoir* in Yuma County, near the Colorado-Kansas line, about 30 miles north of Burlington.

A good number of 3½- to 5-pound fish are caught annually, plus a few up to 6 pounds; and the best fishing is usually from mid-April to mid-June. The largest bass ever reported from the reservoir weighed 7 pounds and 3 ounces.

Fishery officials say Bonny has a stable water level throughout the year, compared to some other state waters, and consequently Bonny's bass show better growth.

Anglers fishing here should concentrate on the edges of the weedbeds early and late in the day, shifting to deeper water during midday. Two areas of the lake which seem to regularly produce bass are the rocky riprap along the dam and the region of North Cove. Fish in May and early June if you want to be there when the action peaks.

Bonny is subject to occasional high winds, and fishing can be difficult during the blows.

Meals and motel lodging can be located at the town of Idalia, some 12 miles from the lake. The lake itself offers three boat ramps, bait and tackle supplies, and rental boats. An overnight or seasonal permit is required to stay in the Bonny Lake campground.

The Colorado Department of Game, Fish, and Parks can provide additional information. The address is 6060 Broadway, Denver, Colorado 80216.

Idaho

One of the best bets for Idaho bassers is smallmouth bass fishing in the main branch of the *Snake River*. A fair number of 3- to 4-pound bass and an occasional 5-pounder are taken in the area of the Snake about 60 miles west of Boise, on the Idaho-Oregon border. U.S. Highway 95 services the area from north and south, while Interstate 80 brings in east and westbound fishermen.

April and May produce some topnotch smallmouth action to anglers float fishing the riffle areas. Look for the fish along undercut banks or in pockets of boulders. Use shiny spinning lures, a small jig, or a live nightcrawler with a light spinning outfit.

Free public launching sites can be found at Olds Ferry, west of the town of Weiser, or near the town of Marsing on U.S. 95. Combinations down to a 12-foot boat and 10-horsepower can be used in the slower moving parts of the Snake.

Accommodations in the area include restaurants and motels in Weiser, Payette, and Marsing. There are also good campgrounds located at nearby Brownlee Reservoir, Marsing, and, on the Oregon side of the river, near Weiser.

For more information write: Idaho Department of Fish and Game, 600 S. Walnut, Box 25, Boise, Idaho 83707.

A school-sized bass is "lipped" by angler on the sprawling waters of Lake Powell.

Montana

Good bass fishing in Montana, a state famous for its blue-ribbon trout angling? Well, *Ninepipe Reservoir*, in the northwest area of the state, is indeed a respectable bass fishery. Located about 5 miles south of Ronan, on U.S. Highway 93, the lake is part of the Ninepipe National Wildlife Refuge and offers only shore fishing and wading (no boats are allowed). A 6- or 7-pound bass is considered tops in Ninepipe.

The reservoir is created by the damming of several creeks and streams in the Mission Valley. Since it is located on the Flathead Indian Reservation, a $3-per-day use permit or a $5 year-long permit is required. Permits can be obtained in several stores in the nearby towns of Ronan and St. Ignatius.

Many fishermen fling plastic worms into the relatively shallow lake. Black and purple are considered to be the best worm colors. In the summer, the best fishing period, spinnerbaits and surface plugs also work well. At times the bass will hold in the irrigation channels in the lake, and anglers must wade to reach these spots.

St. Ignatius is located 7 miles south of Ninepipe on Montana Highway

93 and offers motels and meals, as well as fishing tackle, gas, and other supplies. Similar services can be found at Ronan, 5 miles north of the lake.

One good source of current fishing information is Ronan Sporting Goods, Box 8, Ronan, Montana 59864.

Nevada

Nevada bass anglers have 67-mile-long *Lake Mohave* in the extreme southern part of the state, which holds some good bass in the 5- to 10-pound class. Formed by the Colorado River, Lake Mohave creates part of the Nevada-Arizona boundary and ranges from Boulder Dam on the north to Davis Dam on the south. One of the larger lakes of the West, Mohave holds over 1,800,000 acre feet of water at full capacity.

There are three major marinas on the lake, and all contain full services (launch ramps, motels, campgrounds, restaurants, marine supplies, tackle, bait, boat slips, and so forth). Two marinas are located in the "bass areas" of the lake—Cottonwood Cove Resort in the midsection of Mohave and Lake Mohave Resort to the far south. Willow Beach Resort, at the north-

These anglers try a cove on Lake Mohave.

ern end of the lake, fronts on the "river" portion of the lake where trout fishing dominates.

The Nevada state-record bass was taken at Lake Mohave in 1972 when an 11-pound fish was landed. Several bass clubs hold tournaments on the lake, and it regularly produces 3- to 8-pound bass for the better fishermen, especially in spring and winter.

Generally, some of the best fishing occurs about 2 to 15 miles north of Cottonwood Cove Resort and also to the south, from the narrows down to Davis Dam. Anglers regularly use plastic worms, crankplugs, live waterdogs, nightcrawlers, spinnerbaits, and leadhead jigs.

High winds can plague this desert lake, but fine fishing can result when weather conditions are good. I know one angler who fished the lake 10 times in 1977 and caught 15 to 40 bass each trip. Many of the fish he kept were in the 5- to 7-pound category. And a few years ago, my father-in-law took a 9¼-pound bass out of Mohave, using a live waterdog for bait.

For more information about Lake Mohave write: Lake Mohave Resort, Davis Dam, Bullhead City, Arizona 86430; or Cottonwood Cove Resort, Box 123, Searchlight, Nevada 89046. Current fishing condition informa-

Working a plastic worm over a bottom structure, this Western bass angler watches his line for signs of a strike.

tion for the Cottonwood Cove area may be obtained from Searchlight Bait and Storage, Box 291, Searchlight, Nevada 89046 [phone (702) 297-1423].

New Mexico

Ute Lake in northeastern New Mexico holds the state records for both largemouth bass (11 pounds) and smallmouth bass (6 pounds, 9 ounces). Near the town of Logan, Ute is formed by the backup of the Canadian River and contains about 4,000 surface acres when full.

Since Ute is little affected by water level changes, it produces fairly good catches of 4- to 5-pound largemouths and some 2- to 3-pound small-mouths. April and August are two of the best months for bass.

Ute's rocky bluffs and points hold a good percentage of the larger fish, but other nice catches can be taken on underwater structure located with a depthfinder. Plastic worms, spinnerbaits, leadhead jigs, and crankplugs all take a share of the fish.

Visitors will find a campground at the reservoir, plus a marina, boat and motor rentals, launchramps, and tackle and grocery supplies.

The New Mexico Department of Game and Fish, State Capitol, Santa Fe, New Mexico 87501, can supply more information on Ute Lake. You may also wish to write the State Parks Commission, Santa Fe, New Mexico 87501.

Oregon

April, May and June produce some noteworthy catches of 2- to 4-pound bass at *Owyhee Reservoir* in southeastern Oregon, and anglers may occasionally hook a 5- to 6-pounder. Off State Highway 201, some 33 miles southwest of Nyssa, the reservoir is a 12,000 surface acre impound-ment with varying shoreline habitat.

Some of the best catches are traditionally taken along the regions of steep, rocky bluffs or from shoreline areas containing broken rocks and boulders. Sources at the lake say the usual variety of bass lures and baits will work here, with no one type outstanding.

There are three visitor service areas at the lake (Leslie Gulch, Owyhee Lake Resort, and Gordon Creek) and several launching sites, as well as a state park campground. Available are fishing supplies, gas, rental boats, food, and picnic areas.

Two good sources for Owyhee Reservoir information are: Oregon State Marine Board, 3000 Market Street N.E., No. 505, Salem, Oregon 97310; and Travel Information Section, 101 State Highway Building, Salem, Oregon 97310.

Utah

Utah contains what has become one of the best bass fishing lakes in the West, sprawling *Lake Powell*, in the southeastern part of the state. Powell is huge: 1,980 miles of shoreline (more than the entire Western Pacific Coast) ringing a lake which is 186 miles long and contains 91 major side canyons, coves, and river arms.

The largest bass taken at Lake Powell to date weighed 10 pounds and 2 ounces; more commonly the lake produces excellent catches of 2- to 3- pound fish. Because of an abundant population of threadfin shad, the main forage base for bass, Powell's largemouths have multiplied to a healthy fishery which extends virtually the length of the reservoir.

Some of the best fishing areas are the San Juan River arm, the Escalante River, Iceberg Canyon, Dangling Rope Canyon, and the northern region of the lake approaching Hite. This lake is so large that marinas are located about 50 miles apart; therefore, fishermen must pay attention to their fuel supplies when traveling the lake.

The spring (March through early May) and fall (October through mid-November) produce some of the hottest bass fishing, and live waterdogs are a prime bait. Plastic worms, leadhead jigs, and crankplugs also work well. Bass seem to prefer points of land and rockslides at Powell, although they will be caught back in the coves in the spring.

The five major marinas on the lake offer good facilities, and three of them (Wahweap, Hall's Crossing, and Bullfrog) offer full services including campgrounds, boat ramps, food, motel lodging, boat slips, bait and tackle, RV areas, marine supplies, trailer parks, and licensed fishing guide service.

Additional information regarding Lake Powell fishing and accommodations may be obtained by writing: Wahweap Lodge and Marina, Box 1597, Page, Arizona 86040; Bullfrog Marina, 231 East Fourth South, Salt Lake City, Utah 84111; and Hall's Crossing Marina, Lake Powell Ferry Service, Inc., Blanding, Utah 84511.

Washington

Banks Lake, in the Columbia Basin of Washington, yields a good number of 3- to 5-pound bass annually, plus a few larger fish up to 8 pounds. The reservoir, in fact, produced a new state-record bass (11 pounds, 9 ounces) in 1977. The lake is reached via U.S. Highway 2.

Banks Lake has relatively warm water temperatures for most of the year, encouraging its production of hefty bass. Forage fish also abound in the lake—young perch, crappie, and even small, planted salmon and trout which the bass eat.

Many Washington anglers prefer crankplugs and plastic worms at this lake. There are several rocky points, dropoffs, and underwater ledges

The end of a good day of bass fishing.

which seem to hold the larger fish. Since there isn't a lot of topwater vegetation, surface lures are seldom used here.

This popular reservoir is situated in Steamboat Rock State Park, where facilities include over 100 full hookup campsites, a swimming beach, boat launching ramps, and a day-use area. People wishing other accommodations will find motels in the nearby towns.

More fishing information may be obtained by writing: Grant County Chamber of Commerce, Ephrata, Washington 98823.

Wyoming

There's more than fabulous trout fishing in Wyoming—at least at *Ocean Lake*, located in the central part of the Cowboy State. Ocean Lake offers some respectable fishing for largemouth bass, and while "trophy" size fish here are considerably smaller than their southern counterparts, the reservoir does supply enough 2- to 3-pounders to make angling interesting. The largest bass taken here so far was in the 5-pound class.

Situated about 17 miles northwest of Riverton, Ocean Lake is fed by a series of 19 inlet drainage ditches, holds in excess of 6,000 surface acres of water when full, and has a maximum depth of 26 feet.

Bass anglers fish two principal types of habitat at Ocean—areas of shoreline vegetation and spots containing a shale bottom—and action usually peaks from mid-May until late June. Spinnerbaits, plastic worms, crankplugs, and small jigs rank as the best lures at this warmwater fishery.

At the site are three launch ramps, plus cabin rentals, rental boats, and fishing supplies. The lake can be reached from state secondary Highways 134 and 133 which border the lake or from U.S. Highway 26.

More information concerning Ocean Lake can be obtained by writing the Wyoming Game and Fish Department, Box 1589, Cheyenne, Wyoming 92001.

8

In Search of Superbass

Right now, there is probably a largemouth bass swimming in a Western lake that would fulfill the dream of any bass fisherman. The fish I'm speaking of is not the largest bass in California nor the largest bass in the West nor the largest bass in the nation.

It is the largest bass *in the world*.

It is a fish that is larger than the current world-record largemouth bass —a 22-pound, 4-ounce giant caught in 1932 by George W. Perry at Montgomery Lake, Georgia.

There could, in fact, be more than one mammoth *Micropterus* larger than Perry's long-celebrated catch now finning in a San Diego County reservoir, for a chain of lakes in that Southern California region has been stocked with the famous Florida-strain of largemouth bass.

That potential world-record bass wouldn't be residing in the far West if this breed of superbass hadn't been transplanted to California as part of a progressive and experimental fish-stocking program. The program began in the late 1950s when some San Diego bass fishermen began to wonder if bass from Florida, where the largemouths achieve big sizes, would adapt successfully to San Diego waters. In Florida, the combination of a nearly-year-around growing season and warm, shallow, aquatically fertile lakes favored growth of the species, and some anglers speculated that San Diego lakes offered a similar environment. So why wouldn't Florida bass do just as well out West?

The California Department of Fish and Game began to ponder that question, too, and in May 1959 through an arrangement of the City and County of San Diego and the Florida and California fish and game departments, the first Floridas came to the Golden State. A plane with 20,000 passengers (fingerling bass) reared at a Florida hatchery took off from a Pensacola runway and landed out West.

The California Department of Fish and Game had already prepared a

*California's largest superbass to date, this
20-pound, 15-ounce giant was caught at San Diego's
Lake Miramar by Dave Zimmerlee.*

home for the new arrivals at Upper Otay Reservoir in San Diego County. The DFG first treated Upper Otay with rotenone, a chemical which eliminated all previously existing fish so that the lake could contain only Floridas. Then threadfin shad were added to the water to provide food for the airlifted bass. The Floridas went into the lake, carried off their first successful spawn in the spring of 1960, and have felt at home ever since.

With fish out of Upper Otay, the stocking of other lakes began.

In 1960, lakes Wohlford, Sutherland, and Lower Otay received Florida bass, followed in 1961 by plants in Lake Miramar and El Capitan Lake. The new program was expanded in 1962 when Floridas entered the waters of Lake Henshaw. More recently, the superbass were added to San Vicente Lake in 1969 and Lake Murray in 1972.

For the first six years of the experiment, there was little encouraging news; short-term, comparative-growth studies in California and Florida indicated *no* significant size differences between Florida and northern bass for comparably old fish. It appeared that the attempt to produce trophy fishing might fail, and the long-standing California state record of 14 pounds for a northern bass taken at Round Valley Reservoir in 1948 would stand for a long, long time.

But in 1966, some remarkable changes began to appear. Using tagged-fish studies to measure bass growth, DFG biologists began to notice that in El Capitan Lake, Florida bass only 7 years old had reached weights of 9 to 11 pounds! That same year, a 13-pound Florida bass was landed at Lake Wohlford, setting a new San Diego County record.

In 1968, the California record was toppled, not once but twice, when Lake Wohlford yielded Florida bass weighing 14 pounds and 9 ounces, then 14 pounds and 15 ounces.

The new state record lasted only a year.

In April, 1969, Miramar Reservoir rewarded a fisherman with a 15-pound, 4-ounce Florida.

Although no new state record was set in 1970, Lake Wohlford did produce a floating, dead bass which tipped the scales at 16 pounds and 15 ounces, and a poacher, fishing out of season at Lower Otay Lake, caught an unofficial 15-pound, 7¾-ounce Florida transplant.

Not only were the Florida bass growing remarkably large, but they were growing in number, too. In 1971, for instance, a total of 201 known bass *over 9 pounds* each was recorded at San Diego lakes during a 10-month period from January 1 to November 1. A 16-pound, 11-ounce trophy was pulled out of Miramar Lake, again toppling the existing state record. Again, the new record lasted but a year.

In July of 1972, James A. Bates of Chula Vista flipped out a plastic worm at Lake Murray; when the lure came back, it was stuck in the jaws of a 17-pound, 14-ounce Florida.

Two years passed, and then the second largest bass ever caught in the world was hooked at Lake Miramar. Dave Zimmerlee of San Diego dangled a live nightcrawler in front of the fish and set a new California record when the 20-pound, 15-ounce Gargantuan catch was weighed.

Today, there is no doubt that an outstanding trophy fishery for large-mouth bass has been established in San Diego waters. And while Zimmerlee's nearly 21-pound fish hasn't been topped (at this writing), there have been some other interesting developments.

One is that one of the newest Florida bass lakes, San Vicente, which only received the famous fish in 1969, is now producing some of the fastest growing lunkers.

"San Vicente bass show an excellent growth rate and excellent health conditions because of the trout they feed on," says Larry Bottroff, a California Department of Fish and Game fishery biologist and a recognized expert on the Florida bass transplant program. "The growth rate of Floridas in San Vicente appears to be much better than our other [San Diego] trout lakes. In a shorter time, San Vicente has produced bigger fish."

The lake records reveal just how productive San Vicente is for large bass. From October 1975 to July 1976, for example, the reservoir yielded 138 bass weighing *over 6 pounds* each. The monthly breakdown for 6-pound-plus bass showed: October 1975, 15 fish; November, 6 fish; December, 2 fish; January 1976, 6 fish; February, 14 fish; March, 42 fish; April, 41 fish; May, 11; June, 2; July, 2.

In March and April alone, 83 lunker bass were caught at the lake, including 11 over 6 pounds, 18 over 7 pounds, 13 over 8 pounds, 15 over 9 pounds, 15 over 10 pounds, 4 in the 11-pound class, 3 over 12 pounds, a 13-pounder and 14-pounder, a pair in the 16-pound category, an an 18-pounder.

The 18-pound, 9-ounce monster taken by Bob Sandberg was estimated to be only 9 or 10 years old, raising speculation that the lake could produce the Grandest Fish of All.

San Vicente also produced a new California state-record *bass limit* (5 fish) early in 1976 when Jim Phelps of Escondido used live waterdogs for bait and took an incredible stringer of Floridas weighing 13 pounds and 3 ounces, 9 pounds and 10 ounces, 9 pounds and 2 ounces, 7 pounds and 6 ounces, and 4 pounds and 9 ounces. Totaling 43 pounds and 14 ounces of bass, his catch averaged over 8 pounds per fish!

Bill Murphy of Santee also enjoyed some fabulous trophy fishing at San Vicente in the fall of 1976. In the first month of the season there, he took more large bass than some anglers catch in their lifetimes. In pounds and ounces, Murphy's harvest included bass weighing: 13-6, 11-15, 11-7, 10-11, 10-7, 10-5, 8-9, 8-6, 7-15, 7-0, 6-12, 6-12, 6-4 and "some others," he says, "that I lost track of."

Murphy takes many of his large bass on live crawdads, using 10-pound test line in the wintertime and 12-pound test in the summertime. He also likes plastic worms in the late spring and late fall and concentrates on 12- to 25-foot depths.

The evidence seems to indicate that there is one helluva fish somewhere in one of the San Diego lakes, according to local observers.

JIM BROWN, lakes specialist with the San Diego City Lakes Department: "I feel there may be a new world record in *both* San Vicente and Miramar lakes. In 1975, a utilities department supervisor was diving at Lake Miramar and spotted *three* huge bass near the water outlet tower. He is an experienced diver and knows the sizes of fish, particularly because he has done extensive work on the City's reservoirs. He felt all three were potential world records."

MIKE LEMBECK, fishery biologist: "There could be a world record in any of four San Diego lakes right now—Miramar, Wohlford, Murray, or San Vicente—because fish weighing from 16 pounds, 15 ounces to 20 pounds, 15 ounces have been verified at these lakes from 1970 to 1976." Lembeck believes that if a new world record comes from San Vicente, it will most probably be taken on a live bait, a crawdad, waterdog, or nightcrawler. He says there's a good chance the celebrated fish will be caught on 10- to 15-pound test line "by anchoring over a structure spot or drifting a live bait in 10 to 25 feet of water."

BILL JACKSON, El Cajon, local skilled fisherman: "I've seen bass in San Vicente Lake during the spawning season that are mammoth. They're very spooky. To see them you have to use your trolling motor to creep up to the spots and then lay down in the front of your boat and use polaroid sunglasses to see through the water.

"There are places in San Vicente where these big fish spawn every year; and since I've been fishing there, I've only hooked one. I'm talking about bass weighing *over 20 pounds*. I hate to admit it, but I lost that fish after fighting it for about 5 minutes on 8-pound test line. It made four runs and jumped twice before it got away."

BOB SANDBERG, San Diego, local skilled angler: "While working with the fish and game department about four years ago, I saw a bass near the face of the dam at Lake Miramar. I'd estimate its size at 23 or 24 pounds."

A lot has happened since that planeload of fingerling bass took off from Florida and landed in California. The introduction of Florida bass into San Diego waters has been a resounding success in terms of big fish, and anglers in search of a superbass may soon bring the world record out West.

Feel lucky?

Larry Hopper is one of the highest-ranking members of the Western Bass Fishing Association.

9

A Western Pro Talks Bass

If you had the opportunity to spend a few hours with one of the finest bass fishermen in the West, asking him any questions you wanted about bass fishing, you'd probably learn a lot about improving your own angling skills. I had this opportunity while interviewing a professional tournament bass angler for an article which appeared recently in *Western Outdoors* magazine.

Larry Hopper of Santa Ana, California, is a member of the Western Bass Fishing Association and has finished first in three WBFA tournaments in the past 2 years, as well as placed among the top 10 tourney anglers in several other tourneys. In 1974, he ranked sixth overall in WBFA tournament point standings, improving that position to second overall in both 1975 and 1976. An extremely skilled fisherman, Hopper is tournament-sponsored by the Quick Corporation of America, a large fishing tackle manufacturing firm.

Hopper's responses to my question-and-answer interview follow:

GARRISON: What is the first thing you would recommend to a person who is getting started in bass fishing?

HOPPER: You've got to start with basics, otherwise it's easy to get confused over all the theories and all the tackle available. And it's easy to get impatient. You've got to have a system.

First, I'd start off by fishing only one or two lakes. Fish those lakes until you *know* them well, until you understand all the shoreline features of that lake—where the deep water is, and where most of the bass are caught. It's a lot harder to begin learning about bass fishing by jumping around from lake to lake, so begin with just one or two, because each lake is different.

GARRISON: Let's say a guy wants to buy a first, basic bass-fishing outfit. What would you recommend?

HOPPER: I'd recommend spinning equipment. Buy a 5½- or 6-foot spinning rod, medium-action, fast taper, and a medium-size, open-face spinning reel, and use 10-pound test line. That's a good beginning. This outfit will cast reasonable distances, will handle a big bass fairly well and, being spinning tackle, it won't bog down a beginner with the backlashes he can get from bait-casting tackle. Still, once he's developed some skills, he should add bait-casting gear to his equipment.

GARRISON: How about fishing lures?

HOPPER: A lot of would-be bass fishermen make a mistake in stuffing their boxes with all types of lures, and they keep looking for a secret to success in their tackle box. They spend all their time changing lures. A lot of people would improve their catches if they just stuck to four basic lure types: the crankplug, spinnerbait, plastic worm, and leadhead jig.

GARRISON: Why these lures?

HOPPER: They are all proven fish catchers. The crankplug and the spinnerbait work extremely well in the shallows and down to moderate depths, while the plastic worm and leadhead jig are two of the most versatile lures ever produced; by scaling down their size and weight they can be fished shallow; and the larger heavier ones can be fished deep.

These four lure designs can be fished very slow (the plastic worm, spinnerbait, and leadhead) to very fast (the crankplug and spinnerbait). The spinnerbait also makes an excellent *flutter* lure; that is, a lot of times bass will hit it as the blades are fluttering while it's sinking. Each of these lures also has a different shape and action, so you can cover a lot of fish preferences with just four types of artificials.

GARRISON: Don't you think there're a lot of people who have fished with plastic worms but never really mastered them?

HOPPER: That's true. The worm takes patience to fish properly. I still see fishermen rigging the worm in a bad way; they should probably be rigging it Texas-style, in which the hook point comes out of the top of the plastic worm and then is reinserted into the body of the worm. If anyone reads this story and doesn't know what the Texas-style, weedless rigging means, I'd suggest he ask a good bass fisherman or ask at a tackle store. Usually, if he doesn't rig it weedless, he'll spend lots of time hung up on brush and then get disenchanted with plastic worm fishing and give it up.

GARRISON: What other mistakes do you see anglers commit while fishing a plastic worm?

HOPPER: Believe it or not, I still see some fishermen casting out a plastic worm and then reeling it in before it ever settles to the bottom. The worm *has to be down*—bumping the bottom—if it's going to be effective. And it's got to be retrieved *very slowly*, using short twitches of the rod tip. As an example, a 40- or 50-foot cast with a crankplug might take less than 30 seconds to retrieve, but a 40- or 50-foot cast with a plastic worm will take 2 to 3 minutes, maybe more, to retrieve properly. The worm has to look natural to a bass; and a natural worm doesn't zip through the water, it crawls.

Another thing that you've got to learn about plastic worm or leadhead jig fishing is that you've got to be able to *feel* what the lure is going over on the bottom. One simple way to do that is to find a shallow, clear-water area where you can see the structure on the bottom—the brush, rocks, boulders, trees, and so forth. Cast the lure so it can be retrieved back through the rocks or brush, then close your eyes and *feel* the sensation this sends through the line and the rod tip. You should repeat this until you can tell the difference between the feel of rocks and brush. Then, when you go out in deeper or off-color water, you'll be fishing, figuratively, with your eyes closed.

GARRISON: What does a bass feel like when it hits a plastic worm?

HOPPER: For one thing, it doesn't feel like rocks or brush; that's why it's so important to learn the feel of the lure on the bottom. A bass strike is usually more of a sharp rap or twitch along the line. It's very faint, but very distinct. Once you learn to feel the bottom, there's no mistaking it.

You've also got to *watch* your line all the time you're fishing a worm or a leadhead. Lots of times the line will twitch, signaling a strike. If you're not watching your line for those twitches, which usually come when the lure is sinking or at rest, you'll probably miss at least half the strikes.

GARRISON: Then when do you set the hook?

HOPPER: If I were talking to a beginner, I'd say about 2 to 3 seconds after I felt the strike. Just lower the rod tip to about 9 o'clock, reel in any slack in the line, and then strike *sharply* by heaving the rod up to 11 or 12 o'clock. You don't have to go farther back with the rod tip, but you do have to strike forcefully because you have to drive the hook point the rest of the way through the worm and into the bass' mouth.

GARRISON: If you don't solidly drive the hook point in the fish, it may throw the lure free when it jumps.

HOPPER: Right. In fact, that's one of the chief causes of beginners losing bass.

GARRISON: What are some other causes of lost fish?

HOPPER: Slack in the line makes it much easier for the fish to shake his head or jump and throw the hook, and that's with any type of lure. Another cause is a guy getting so excited when the fish gets near the boat that he tightens up the reel drag or clamps his thumb on the reel spool when the fish gets close and tries to make another run or two. Often, a bass seems to get recharged when it gets near the boat, and you've got to be prepared for that.

GARRISON: Let's say the occasional bass fisherman doesn't own a depthfinder. What kinds of visible shoreline features would you tell him to fish?

HOPPER: If I could pick just two to fish, I'd fish areas of brush and points of land that dip into the water. There are *always* some fish shallow in brush, and these fish are usually biters. The same is true for points. If you're starting out, stick to points and brush and you'll catch some fish, especially if you use a percentage lure, and you'll also learn a lot about bass fishing.

GARRISON: You said "percentage lure." What do you mean?

HOPPER: A spinnerbait or crankplug is a percentage lure; in other words, if you make a lot of casts with them, you'll catch a certain percentage of fish. They are both pitch-and-crank lures—you cast them out and just wind them in, although there are some variations on this. The important thing is that they are easy to use; they cast well, have a built-in action, and the only skill really required to retrieve them properly is the ability to turn the reel handle. Since they can be fished fast, you can cover a lot of water in a short time, and that's important in locating bass. In fact, the spinnerbait and crankplug are two of the easiest, yet most effective lures for a learning bass fisherman to use.

GARRISON: How important is accurate casting in bass fishing?

HOPPER: About like learning to crawl before you walk. If you can't cast accurately, you won't consistently catch bass. And that's important, because poor casting is a common weakness of would-be bass fishermen. If you're target casting to shoreline structure, casting to objects you can see, you've got to be able to put your lure fairly close to that tree stump or piece of brush or rocky ledge. Bass have a habit of holding tight to structures like these and usually won't move more than a few feet to strike.

GARRISON: Isn't it sometimes better to cast beyond the actual target?

HOPPER: Yes, if you're casting to a stump, a boulder, old dock pilings, brush, and such, you should actually cast so that the lure falls 4 to 6 feet *behind* the target. That way it won't fall on top of a fish and spook it; it will land beyond the fish and will be passing by the fish when it's got some action to it. If the water's shallow, the lure should be a smaller, lighter one, too, so it doesn't crash into the water but just sort of plops. A bass meal falling into the water doesn't crash. And bass know it.

GARRISON: Speaking of spooking bass, how important is it to be quiet when approaching the fishing spot?

HOPPER: It's so important that pro bass fishermen use electric trolling motors to eliminate a lot of maneuvering noise. They also avoid shuffling tackle boxes and banging things around in their boat. And, when fishing clear water, they'll stay farther away from these spots—just about the distance of their longest possible casts. Any fisherman, pro or occasional, should avoid boat noises, keep a low silhouette, and avoid running in on a spot while the big motor is going. I'm talking about shallow water, down to about 25 feet. I don't think it's as important when fishing deeper, unless the water is extremely clear.

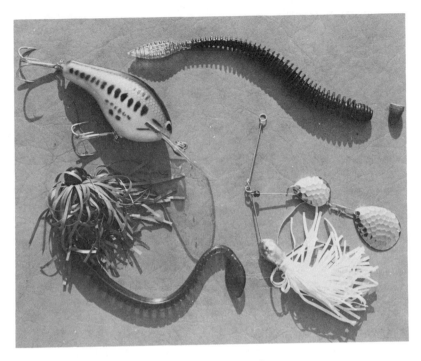

These are Larry Hopper's four basic choices in lures:
(clockwise from upper left) crankplug, plastic worm,
spinnerbait, and leadhead jig.

GARRISON: Do you feel the mental aspects of bass fishing are under-estimated?

HOPPER: Sometimes I think they are more than underestimated. You hear a lot about what lure to use or what depth to fish or what depthfinder is best, but you hear very little about two of the most important things which aren't found in a tackle box: persistence and confidence.

GARRISON: Can you be more specific?

HOPPER: You've got to tell yourself you're going to catch fish before you make your first cast of the day. Then you've got to have the confidence to know you really will. I've fished lots of tournaments when I started off slow; in fact, a lot of occasional fishermen would have probably just quit, saying, "The fish aren't biting today." But there're darned few days when bass won't bite to some degree; you just have to find what they want, what kind of territory they are in that day, and at what depth.

You want a good example of persistence? A serious bass fisherman will get out on the water at the crack of dawn and will be prepared to stay until dark or at least until the lake closes. Now the average guy—say, using a crankplug—may try several fishing spots and catch nothing, so he slows down in both effort and enthusiasm. His casts get sloppier and he falls into the trap of thinking about quitting. He takes an hour for lunch and maybe even takes a nap. By the end of his fishing day, which may be the middle of the afternoon, he's made 200 to 300 casts.

The serious bass fisherman never quits. Sometimes he doesn't even stop for lunch. He casts and retrieves and casts and retrieves and casts and retrieves, because he has persistence. He knows sooner or later he'll find fish. He doesn't lose time backlashing, and he puts his lure on target with no wasted effort. Before he leaves the spot he's fishing, he already knows the next spot he's going to fish and starts casting there before the boat even settles to a full stop. By the end of his fishing day he's made maybe 1,000 to 1,500 casts.

Now, just compare 300 casts to 1,500 casts and you can see that the skillful bass guy fishes five days to the average guy's one, all in the same day. No wonder the pro catches more fish. Part of his "luck" is merely a function of how many casts he makes, how many times his lure runs through the water.

GARRISON: What boat accessory gear do you feel is basic for the good bass angler?

HOPPER: If you are asking what pieces of equipment will most improve his catches without really loading the boat, I'd say a depthfinder, a trolling motor, and two anchors. He should at least have a basic, portable depthfinder if he fishes from a rental boat. Knowing the depth and the type of bottom terrain are critical to taking consistently good catches, and only a depthfinder tells you that. A trolling motor's good for sneaking up on fishing spots and for holding a boat steady in the wind. And if a guy wants to fish a spot awhile with plastic worms or even live bait, he should have a bow and a stern anchor so the boat won't swing.

GARRISON: What do you consider your single most important asset as an expert bass fisherman?

HOPPER: Well, first, I don't know if any of us are experts. Some of us just seem to do better, I guess. Anyway, this sounds like a cop-out, but I'd say *experience*. You only get a lot of experience by fishing a lot. And experience tells you what lures and what depths to match to a certain set of conditions. You can look back and remember that you caught fish at a certain lake in July, and you caught them perhaps 12 to 18 feet deep around brush, on purple plastic worms. When you've done that a few times, you remember to match up all those factors and you find it often works again.

GARRISON: Would it be a good idea, then, for a fisherman to keep a log?

HOPPER: Definitely, at least for quite awhile. I kept a fishing log for years, but now I've reached the point at which I usually remember without referring to a log. But a log kept up accurately—listing dates, places, best areas, best times of day, lures, sizes of fish, and other data—can be a great learning aid, especially after a guy has two or three years' worth of material in it. Then he can really start comparing.

GARRISON: How long should a learning bass fisherman try a certain fishing spot?

HOPPER: Well, if it's a piece of brush or a tree, a small object, probably not more than two or three casts. If you're talking about sitting on a particular point or fishing a larger area of an island or a cove, probably not more than 10 or 15 minutes. I like to keep trying different spots, rather than stay in one place and hope the bass will come to me.

GARRISON: If you have one piece of advice to offer from the experience you've gained, what would it be?

HOPPER: I guess it would be to learn all you can about bass habits and bass structure. Learn where a bass lives and why he lives there. Besides putting in time on the water, there're other ways to learn this. You can attend one of the many, fine bass fishing seminars now held all over this state and in other Western states, or you can talk to buddies who are good bass fishermen. There's also education to be picked up talking to knowledgeable people who work in sporting-goods stores or tackle shops, especially those which carry a big, bass-fishing tackle inventory. You can also read books and join a bass club. The exchange of knowledge and ideas is astounding in many clubs.

GARRISON: Is there anything else you'd like to add?

HOPPER: Maybe I should say this: Bass fishing is what you make it, like most other things in life. To me, it's a challenge. If you work hard at it —and fishing really isn't work in that sense anyway—and you give it a worthwhile effort, you can become about as good as you want. But nobody yet has figured out how to catch a limit every time and, frankly, I hope no one ever does. That, I'm afraid, would take all of the fun and intrigue out of the game.

Good fishing photos are created, not just snapped.

10

For Better Bass Photos

Have you ever caught a bass twice, yet only *hooked* it once?

I'll bet a lot of you have, but you've never really thought about it that way. You caught the fish the first time when you lifted it out of the water in the landing net. Then you captured it again on film when you snapped a photo. I've seen thousands of fishing pictures and noted that many of them fall into one stereotyped category: the typical "dead fish" shot.

We've all seen them. Remember that photo of Harry holding his big fish crosswise across his chest like a piece of cord wood and Harry staring blankly into the camera lens? Chances are he's got a cap on, cloaking his face in shadow, and even the fish may be half hidden because there is little or no contrast between Harry's shirt and the coloring of his catch. If Harry smokes, he's probably got a smoldering cigarette dangling from his lips. And what's that? Why, Harry's got a tree growing straight out his head!

A lot of photos come out that way because the camera operator never stopped to consider what makes a better picture. "Snapshot" is a truly descriptive term; a snapshot is the result of somebody snapping the shutter release without thinking. Good photos are *created*, not just snapped.

Actually, you don't need a sophisticated camera costing several hundred dollars to make more creative, impressive, and pleasing bass fishing photos. Such equipment is indeed necessary for professional work. But the average fisherman can greatly improve his photography in a short time—and while using the popular Instamatic and Polaroid types—if he follows some basic photographic guidelines.

Think about these suggestions the next time you take a camera on a bass fishing trip:

Get rid of camera villains. There are four camera villains that I guard against whenever taking a photo. These distracting or unpleasing elements are sunglasses, hats, cigarettes or cigars, and beverage cans.

Sunglasses are fine for protecting the eyes from the rays of the sun, but they also shield the eyes and part of the face in a photograph, *hiding* the fisherman. Dark sunglasses should come off in a photo. If the sun is especially bright, move your camera subject into light shade or have him turn so the sun is slightly off to one side.

Hats, like sunglasses, can cast dark shadows over the entire head area, especially at midday when the sun is directly overhead and the shadows are straight down. You may clearly "see" your subject even though his face is shaded by a hat, but the camera lens sees with a different "eye"—an eye which must compromise all the brightest and darkest areas in the shot. And chances are good your fisherman's face will be blacked out in shadow if his hat remains.

Sometimes, if the sun is low enough (morning and late afternoon), a hat can remain on the subject's head if the hat is *tilted back* enough to allow light to strike his face.

It's amazing how some of the simplest things in life can be distracting when photographed with a still camera. Things like cigarettes and cigars, dangling from the lips of an angler in a photograph, jump out of the photo at us. The key to taking good photographs is to eliminate all the unnecessary things and to emphasize the *important* things in a picture. And cigarettes aren't necessary—just distracting.

Beverage containers are also distracting, because they are not necessary to the "story" you really want to tell in the photo. You should want to show that Harry caught a beautiful, trophy-size, 9-pound bass; you should not want to show that Harry drinks ABC beer. But what do you think viewers will look at if Harry holds his fish in one hand and the beer can in the other? They'll look at *both*, and the beer can will detract from the impressiveness of the fish.

Watch the background. Keep the background clear and unconfusing. Backgrounds littered with too many objects pull our attention from the center of interest as well as clutter up the photo.

Here are some examples of cluttered backgrounds:

—A sign intruding somewhere in the photo. We've all seen them. They most commonly say something like "Jones Lake Resort," or "No Parking," or "Marina Store." If you really don't want to publicize the regulations or advertise for the resort, eliminate the signs.

—A fisherman and catch, standing in front of his car or truck, with the front fenders of the vehicle taking up the entire width of the photo.

—A group of unrelated people, standing in the background and staring at the camera while the picture is being shot. If you don't look for this when you're taking the photo, you end up with five people in the frame, instead of only the one you wanted.

—Powerlines running through the top portion of the photo where the clear sky should be.

—Trees or powerpoles sprouting from your angler's head. Or subjects with "two bodies" because someone is walking behind your subject when you squeezed the shutter.

What's a good background? Look for something plain: the smooth surface of a bluff or the sky, a *distant* shoreline, the side of a building (a non-distracting wall with no windows, doors, signs, and so forth), or some homogeneous shrubbery.

Remember, too, that as you *increase* the distance between your subject and the background, the background becomes de-emphasized; as you decrease the distance, it becomes emphasized. Taking a picture of your buddy while he's in the boat, with the far shore as a background, will probably have a pleasing effect, but if he has a sanitation truck *directly behind him*, the effect will be much different.

Move in close. Moving in close to your subject is another way to control background (by eliminating it) and to emphasize the important parts of your shot. Ask yourself, "What is it I really want to show in this photo?" Take a minute and think about it. Maybe the answer is, "I want to show Joe, his fish, and the rod and reel he used to catch it." That's fine; move in close with the camera so those are the *only* things emphasized.

Also, you don't have to show *all* of Joe for people to recognize him. That's a common mistake of many shutter snappers.

One good example of a too-far photo is a type I have seen many times. Here's John with his 10-pound bass, and the photographer wanted to get all of John on film, so he took the shot from 20 feet away. Now, what can you see?

First, you can see a guy holding a fish. It looks like John, but you really can't see details of his face from that distance. Second, although he's holding a nice-size fish, you're not really close enough to accurately estimate its weight. Third, you can see that John was wearing yellow tennis shoes, that there was an almost-full trash can 10 feet in front of him, and that the parking lot was well paved, because the expanse of unnecessary foreground in the photo comes between the viewer and the important parts of the shot.

By moving in close, the photographer could prevent all of that distraction.

Remember wanting to show Joe, his fish, and the rod and reel he used to catch it? To take that shot, move in close until the upper edge of the photo will appear just above John's head and the lower edge of the photo will appear just below his waist. Have him hold the fish vertically and with its side to the camera, by slipping his hand under the gillcover on one side of the fish, and have him hold the rod and reel in his other hand. Both the rod and reel and the fish should be in the center portion of the photo. Don't worry about getting the whole rod in the shot; just the reel and handle portion of the rod will tell the story. And holding the fish perfectly sideways will provide good detail of its form.

*Closeup shots focus attention on the main subject of
the photo and direct the viewer's interest. Note the tooth
scars on this crankplug, caused by several hooked fish.*

The object is to practically *fill* the photo with the story-telling objects, allowing just enough space above and below the objects to let the photo "breathe." Giving the viewer only meaningful objects to attract his eyes creates impact.

Stop the blank stares. A lot of fishing photos feature that cold, lifeless, blank stare—an expression most often produced when an angler looks straight ahead into the camera. Now, if a proud angler is holding a trophy fish, why is he looking at the camera? Shouldn't he be admiring his catch? Certainly.

If you have the subject look at his fish, he'll appear more relaxed and "human" in the finished print. Cameras scare some people, but fish don't usually bother them. When the viewer examines the photo and sees the angler looking at his catch, the viewer's eyes will be drawn to the fish, too.

Use comfortable props. Props are things which people in a photo can hold or touch to help them feel more relaxed. Let's say, your buddy just bought a new bass boat rig, and you want to have him and his boat in a picture. If you just have him stand beside the boat, he may assume a stiff, unnatural stance, with both arms hanging straight by his sides. Instead, have him rest a foot on the frame of the boat trailer and use a hand to hold on to the side of the boat. He'll feel more comfortable and look more natural and less like a wanted poster in a post office.

If you're taking a group shot of fishermen, give them all props to hold: a stringer of fish, rod and reel, landing net, tackle box, anything *appropriate* to the photo.

Respect the sun. Except for artificial light, the sun is the main source of illumination for photos. Make proper use of that source. The *basic* rule for fundamental photos is to keep the light behind and over one shoulder of the camera holder. This front-lights the subject and provides good contrast in the shot. Usually, the most pleasing photos are taken when the sun is lower in the sky in the morning and later afternoons. At these lower angles, the sun creates shadows *behind* the camera subjects and improves contrast, instead of casting shadows *down* on the subjects.

Consider contrast. Good contrast is sometimes neglected, producing hard-to-see detail in a photograph. Simply stated, contrast is the amount of difference in black and white tones in a black-and-white photo or in lighter and darker colors in a color photo. Contrast in a photo can be high, medium, or low. You may not be able to control *all* of the contrast, but you can produce good contrast between the important parts of your photo.

Consider what would happen if you took a black-and-white photo of your buddy holding a predominantly green bass in front of his dark blue shirt. When those two colors are converted to their black-and-white tones, the bass will blend into the shirt in one dark, indistinguishable area. If that same fish were held up against a white or gray or yellow shirt, there would be fine contrast between the two, and the catch would clearly appear in the finished print.

Remember, light-colored objects in front of dark objects, and vice versa, produce more contrast. Take a look at what you want to photograph, and then look *beyond* it to determine the contrast effect. You might be able to improve the contrast markedly just by having the subject take off a jacket or hold a fish more to one side so it will be silhouetted by sky or move over a few feet to a different spot.

Shoot for variety. A lot of fishermen never think beyond taking those "dead fish" photos. After you've seen half a dozen of these in an album, all the rest look the same. There're lots of activities associated with bass fishing that many people seldom photograph, yet all make fine pictures. They lend variety to your pictures, tell a more complete story of your trip, and are interesting for friends to view.

Here's some possibilities for activity photos:
- Launching the boat in the morning.
- Your partner releasing a bass back into the lake.
- The man at the wheel operating the boat.
- Closeups of your favorite lures.

- Scenic photos of boat and angler along the shore (taken by camera operator on shore).
- Netting a bass.
- Fisherman with bent rod, fighting a fish.
- Your buddy showing off his catch of fish to another person. ,

Use your candid camera. Some of the best, most natural-looking photos are taken when people don't realize they are being photographed. Candid shots capture genuine expressions and natural body forms—they can also produce some funny shots.

I have one beauty of the posterior end of a fishing buddy who leaned far over the side of the boat, trying to retrieve a cigarette lighter he had dropped. Well, at least *I* think it's funny, even if he doesn't.

Time your shutter release to show water streaming out of the landing net.

*In a good photo the unnecessary objects, such as trash
containers and beer cans, are eliminated so that the viewer can
concentrate on the fisherman and his fish (in this case,
Jim Phelps and his 43-pound, 14-ounce catch).*

A Final Thought

I love to fish.

As an angler, I have sometimes pursued a prize or fished for the table, which does not automatically make one a prostitute in the first case or a meat hunter in the second. It is not always the goal which is inherently wrong; often it is the way that goal is sought.

I never hope to fish purely for units of consumption—whether in pounds for the plate or points for the board—because the outdoors has more satisfying rewards. Its spiritual food is the drinking in of fresh air and the swallowing of beautiful scenes, and its points system recognizes the number of leaves wafting to the water, or the repetitions of the whippoor-will.

In remote places, fishing touches me with that tingling awe of feeling small upon this earth, a feeling which must have been shared by the Ancient Ones.

It is a good sport.

—Chuck Garrison

Acknowledgements

This book could never have been written without the cooperation of the many good fishing friends whom I've met in my profession of outdoor photojournalism—those proficient catchers of fish who, through the years, have unselfishly shared their knowledge and techniques with me, so that I may now share them with you.

In addition, I am grateful to Bob Cobb of the Bass Anglers Sportsman Society (BASS) and Bill Rice of the Western Bass Fishing Association (WBFA) for providing some of the *Introduction* information. A word of thanks is also due George McCammon, Chief of the Inland Fisheries Branch, California Department of Fish and Game, for writing a *Foreword* to this book which gives us an overview of modern Western bass fishing and some of its resource considerations.

Finally, a thank-you goes out to the public information officers of the various Western fish and game departments—those unsung PIOs who continually provide outdoor writers with material vital to our work—for their contributions to the chapter *Best Waters of the West*.

About the Author

A full-time outdoor photojournalist, Chuck Garrison is a native-born Southern Californian who loves fishing and writing about fishing, in that order. In the past nine years he has authored nearly 300 magazine articles (most related to fishing), with credits appearing in publications such as *True*, *Field & Stream*, *Outdoor Life*, *Sports Afield*, *Western Outdoors*, *Salt Water Sportsman*, *Fishing World*, *Motorboat* and some 25 others.

In addition to extensive freelance writing, he currently holds positions as the Pacific Coast editor for *Outdoor Life* magazine, staff writer for *Western Outdoor News*, outdoor editor of the *Anaheim Bulletin*, and outdoor writer for the *Santa Ana Register*. He is an active member of the Outdoor Writers Association of America and the American Society of Journalists and Authors.

Chuck has co-authored three other fishing books, in addition to his own recent *Offshore Fishing in Southern California*, published by Chronicle Books.